CHINA'S CHANGING NUCLEAR POSTURE

Reactions to
the South Asian
Nuclear Tests

Ming Zhang

Carnegie Endowment for International Peace
Washington, D.C.

© 1999 by the
Carnegie Endowment for International Peace
1779 Massachusetts Avenue, N.W.
Washington, D.C. 20036
Tel. (202) 483-7600
Fax. (202) 483-1840

China's Changing Nuclear Posture:
Reactions to the South Asian Nuclear Tests
may be ordered ($9.95 paper) from Carnegie's distributor:
The Brookings Institution Press
Department 029, Washington, D.C. 20042-0029, USA
Tel: 1-800-275-1447 or 202-797-6258
Fax: 202-797-6004
E-mail: bibooks@brook.edu

Edited by Thomas W. Skladony.
Cover by Paddy McLaughlin Concepts & Design.
Cover photo: Nelson-Atkins Museum of Art, Kansas City, Mo.
Printed by Automated Graphic Systems, Inc.

Library of Congress Cataloging-in-Publication Data

Zhang, Ming, 1962-
    China's changing nuclear posture : reactions to the South Asian nuclear
    tests / Ming Zhang.
        p. cm.
    Includes bibliographical references (p.).
    ISBN 0-87003-160-0
    1. China—Military policy. 2. Nuclear weapons—China. 3. Nuclear
weapons—India. 4. Nuclear weapons—Pakistan. I. Title.
UA835.Z43 1999
355.02′17′0951—dc2   99-20341
                                                                  CIP

Contents

Foreword   v

Preface   ix

List of Abbreviations   xiii

1. BACKGROUND   1
   The Current State of Chinese Nuclear Forces   2
   Nuclear Deterrence Strategy   3
   Current Chinese Nuclear Policy   6

2. INDIA'S NUCLEAR TESTS: SINO-INDIAN MUTUAL CONCERNS   9
   Sino-Indian Security Relations, 1949–1998   9
   India's Perception of the Nuclear Threat   12
   The Impact of India's Nuclear Tests on China's National Security   14

3. CHINESE REACTIONS TO THE INDIAN AND PAKISTANI TESTS   19
   China's Internal Debate on Non-Proliferation Issues and Policy   19
   The Official Government Reaction   25
   The PLA Reaction   28
   China's Reaction to the Pakistani Nuclear Tests   30

4. THREE SCENARIOS FOR CHINA'S NUCLEAR DOCTRINE AND NON-PROLIFERATION POLICY   33
   Maintenance of the Status Quo   33
   Nuclear Buildup   42
   Reversal of the Commitment   47

5. IMPLICATIONS OF CHINA'S NUCLEAR POLICY FOR OTHER COUNTRIES   53
   Japan   53
   Russia   54

North Korea   55
United States   56

6. WHAT NEXT?   **59**

NOTES   **63**

Appendix A. China's Participation and Positions   73
Regarding Nuclear Arms Control and
Non-Proliferation Regimes

Appendix B. Ambassador Sha Zukang on the   75
Non-Proliferation Regime

Appendix C. Summary of China's Nuclear Weapons   81
and Policies

About the Author   87

About the Non-Proliferation Project   88

The Carnegie Endowment for International Peace   89

Foreword

Deep in China's Henan province, a hundred miles from the ancient city of Xi'an, the People's Liberation Army guards China's small fleet of intercontinental ballistic missiles. The aging Dong Feng-5 missiles are scattered on their launch pads. They are deployed with their liquid fuel tanks empty and with their 4- and 5-megaton nuclear warheads detached and stored separately. Although each has enough explosive power to vaporize an average city, the force pales in comparison to the 5,500 warheads the United States deploys on its modern, highly accurate missiles, or even to the 144 warheads the United Kingdom carries on its Trident sea-launched ballistic missiles. Of the five recognized nuclear powers (the United States, Russia, Britain, France, and China), China has the oldest, least capable, and most stable nuclear-deterrent force. China deployed the first Dong Feng-5 (or "East Wind") in 1981. Slowly, the fleet has grown to the approximately twenty DF-5 missiles deployed today at Luoning and further north at the Xuanhua military base. For two decades, this atomic arsenal, along with dozens of intermediate- and short-range nuclear missiles and air-dropped bombs, has served China's strategic interests.

But China is stirring. Plans to modernize the missile force are under way. China's military and political leaders want modern, solid-fueled missiles like those deployed by the other nuclear powers, perhaps with multiple warheads atop each missile. The Chinese nuclear force may increase in number and will become more accurate. But the exact characteristics of China's future nuclear forces will depend to a great extent on developments to the south and east of China.

Over the Himalayas, India and Pakistan are also stirring. Nuclear tests rocked the Rajasthan Desert and the Chagai Hills in May 1998. Despite international protests, months of delicate U.S. diplomatic efforts, and a recent warming of relations between the two South

Asian neighbors, government leaders in both India and Pakistan say they plan to deploy nuclear weapons. The exclusive five-member club of nuclear-weapon states may soon add countries six and seven, with serious repercussions for China, a member of the club since its first nuclear test in 1964. Although India remains engaged in a shooting war with Pakistan over the disputed territory of Kashmir, it currently regards China as its main strategic adversary. India has announced plans to renew tests of its Agni missile and to develop a new, longer-range Agni II missile capable of reaching most potential targets in China.

Across the Taiwanese Straits and the Sea of Japan, the United States has encouraged both Japan and Taiwan to develop and deploy ballistic missile defenses. After North Korea launched its Taepo-dong intermediate-range ballistic missile over Japanese territory on August 31, 1998, Japan committed a token one billion yen ($8 million) to missile-defense research. Taiwanese leaders, who had rejected missile defenses as a technical gamble and a budgetary sinkhole, are now reexamining the concept as a means of strengthening political ties to the United States. These mere declarations of intent have provoked powerful condemnation from China. Japan and Taiwan may view their potential deployment purely as a defensive measure (and, in the case of Japan, one aimed more at North Korea than China). But Chinese leaders see these defenses as potentially neutralizing the one military advantage they have, as encouraging Taiwanese independence sentiments and, worse, as symbolic of a new, aggressive U.S.-Japan-Taiwan military posture.

How will these events affect China's nuclear forces? Will we see a measured, relatively nonthreatening modernization consistent with the established Chinese nuclear doctrine of fielding only the minimum necessary nuclear deterrent? Or will the deployments of new DF-31 and DF-41 missiles signal the beginning of a nuclear buildup that could realize the world's worst fears of an aggressive, belligerent China seeking to claim its rightful place in a global struggle for power?

Author and analyst Ming Zhang guides us through the debates and profiles the institutions that will determine China's nuclear future. He tracks the history of China's turbulent relations with India and the reaction of top Chinese political and military leaders to the nuclear shocks of 1998. Despite the initial exchange of harsh retorts between the two Asian powers, Zhang believes that China will likely maintain its current policy of limited nuclear deterrence over the next five years. "Beijing still considers economic development its top priority," he argues. "To achieve a higher level of economic modernization, China needs both time and a stable environment. The Chinese leadership has long decided how to apportion its financial resources between economic development and improvements in its nuclear force." Nor does Zhang believe that China will export its nuclear know-how to its neighbors. "At the same time," he writes, "China seems to believe that it is not in its interest to assist any new nuclear weapons power along its borders, including Pakistan."

Unfortunately, this is merely the most likely scenario. International events and internal power struggles could lead to a more ominous nuclear future. Zhang's discussion of these more troubling possibilities is reinforced by remarks made by Ambassador Sha Zukang, China's leading arms-control official, to the Carnegie International Non-Proliferation Conference held in Washington in January 1999 (included here as Appendix B). Ambassador Sha, who is the director-general of the Department of Arms Control and Disarmament at China's Ministry of Foreign Affairs, warned:

> "If a country, in addition to its offensive power, seeks to develop advanced theater missile defense or even national missile defense in an attempt to attain absolute security and unilateral strategic advantage for itself, other countries will be forced to develop more advanced offensive missiles. This will give rise to a new round of arms race which will be in no one's interest."

Reflecting these possible future confrontations, Zhang details three variations on China's nuclear posture. Relying on extensive interviews conducted in China in late 1998, Zhang provides not only informed estimates of possible force deployments, but a guide to the institutions that will frame the internal Chinese debate. China is just beginning to learn that international security regimes can both favor and constrain Chinese interests, Zhang suggests, and there are important differences in how civilian and military institutions approach these regimes.

In addition to Ambassador Sha's speech, other appendices include background information on China's participation in international non-proliferation regimes, excerpts from the chapter on China in the Carnegie Endowment's *Tracking Nuclear Proliferation, 1998*, and a map of China's key nuclear installations.

Ming Zhang is a consultant to the Non-Proliferation Project at the Carnegie Endowment for International Peace. We are deeply grateful for the insights he has provided in this monograph and in his continuing consultations with the Project.

Joseph Cirincione
Non-Proliferation Project Director

March 1999
Washington, D.C.

Preface

As this monograph went to press, a controversy that may significantly impact Sino-U.S. relations and analyses of China's nuclear posture erupted in Washington following news reports of Chinese nuclear espionage against the United States. While this controversy has been brewing for some time, the recent furor deserves some brief comment.

In the past several years, China reportedly has taken advantage of President Clinton's 1995 decision to deregulate technology exports by purchasing forty-six American-made supercomputers. For the first time, China appears to have gained access to a large number of high-performance computers that could help its military conduct simulated nuclear tests and design smaller and more efficient nuclear weapons—including warheads mounted on missiles capable of reaching the United States.

In 1998, several news media reported that Loral Space & Communications Corporation and Hughes Electronics Corporation may have illegally transferred technology to the Chinese rocket program. In February 1996, the two American firms assisted in an investigation of why a Chinese space launch failed. In the process, they reportedly shared technical information with Chinese rocket scientists without obtaining clearance from U.S. officials. If this information has been acquired by the Chinese military, it could be used to improve China's space-launch vehicle guidance and control systems, thus increasing the accuracy of Chinese nuclear missiles.

Finally, in early 1999, new details emerged in the case of a nuclear scientist at Los Alamos National Laboratory who allegedly passed nuclear secrets to China. The House of Representatives concluded in a 700-page, classified report that the espionage had occurred and that it had harmed U.S. national security. Although the incident took place in the mid-1980s, it was not unearthed until 1995, when

American intelligence agents acquired a top-secret Chinese document specifically mentioning the U.S.-designed W-88 warhead. (The W-88, one of America's most advanced warheads, allows a large yield to be packaged in a small container. Eight to ten W-88 warheads fit atop U.S. Trident II submarine-launched missiles.) Most observers thought that China was not capable of developing this type of small warhead, but experts monitoring recent Chinese nuclear tests have detected characteristics similar to those of the W-88. Thus, it is possible that information obtained illegally from Los Alamos enabled China to achieve such a significant breakthrough.

If these three developments are true, it implies that China has been able to improve the accuracy of its missile guidance and control systems and to develop multiple-warhead missiles in less time than experts predicted. China may have made a qualitative leap in its nuclear-weapons technology.

What remains unclear is whether China has actually developed the multiple, independently targetable reentry vehicles (MIRVs) that the other four nuclear powers deploy on their nuclear missiles. There are some indications that China is testing this capability, but no missiles have actually been deployed with multiple warheads.

China currently has approximately twenty long-range ballistic missiles capable of hitting the United States. It intends to replace or supplement this arsenal with newer, land-based missiles over the next ten years. If equipped with multiple warheads, the arsenal would grow from twenty warheads with payloads in the megaton range to, perhaps, 100 warheads with payloads in the kilotons. In the Chinese view, increasing the number of its missiles would enhance the ability of its nuclear force to survive a nuclear attack and to launch a second strike (thus deterring such an attack in the first place). It does not, however, give China a first-strike capability against the United States. The United States will retain, for the foreseeable future, more destructive nuclear power in one Trident submarine alone than China has in its entire long-range missile fleet (each Trident carries 192 warheads on twenty-four missiles). One U.S. submarine, therefore, is more than adequate to deter or respond to any conceivable Chinese nuclear threat.

These controversies, though politically charged, have not reversed current U.S. policy toward China. President Clinton said recently, "I do not believe that the evidence justifies an isolated, no-contact relationship with China." Dennis Hastert, speaker of the House of Representatives, concurred, noting that, "The more we're involved with China, the better off we are—for us and for China and the Pacific area." U.S.-China military exchanges are likely to continue, including top U.S. defense officials' visits to China and a possible visit to Sandia National Laboratory by Chinese military officers in 1999.

Whatever the eventual outcome of these recent controversies, they have stimulated an important new debate about the current capabilities and future direction of China's nuclear-weapons program. I hope that this brief monograph will give policy makers in the United State and elsewhere both essential information and a fresh perspective on China's changing nuclear posture.

* * *

The original version of this study was presented at the July 16, 1998, conference, "The Impact of the South Asia Nuclear Crisis on the Non-Proliferation Regime," organized by the Carnegie Endowment for International Peace. I am grateful to Joseph Cirincione, director of the Non-Proliferation Project at Carnegie, who encouraged me to undertake this challenging project and whose sound advice contributed much to the final publication.

During my research, I visited many arms-control specialists in Chinese government, military, and academic institutes in Beijing in October 1998. I am grateful to those whom I visited both for the hospitality and for the insights they afforded me, even as I respect their desire to remain anonymous.

Many colleagues in the United States commented on the manuscript in whole or in part, especially Bates Gill, Bonnie Glaser, Brad Roberts, and Karen Sutter. I thank them for constructive criticisms that helped me sharpen and improve my analysis. Jennifer Little, Kathleen Daly, Changsheng Lin, and Monte Bullard provided important research assistance. Toby Dalton of the Carnegie Non-Proliferation Project offered numerous valuable suggestions on matters of substance and style, and his colleague Matthew Rice helped with the tables and map. Thomas W. Skladony edited the text. I appreciate their kind assistance and the good cheer with which it was provided.

I am, of course, fully responsible for the substantive arguments of the study and for any errors it may contain.

I dedicate the work to my son, Oak, and to his generation.

Ming Zhang

March 1999
Oakton, Virginia

List of Abbreviations

AMS	Academy of Military Science
ASEAN	Association of Southeast Asian Nations
BJP	Bharatiya Janata Party
CASS	Chinese Academy of Social Sciences
CBM	confidence-building measure
CDSTIC	China Defense Science and Technology Information Center
CICIR	China Institute of Contemporary International Relations
CIISS	China Institute for International Strategic Studies
COSTIND	Commission of Science, Technology, and Industry for National Defense
CTBT	Comprehensive Test Ban Treaty
CWC	Chemical Weapons Convention
FMCT	Fissile Material Cut-off Treaty
GSD	General Staff Department
IAPCM	Institute of Applied Physics and Computational Mathematics
IAEA	International Atomic Energy Agency
ICBM	intercontinental ballistic missile
IRBM	intermediate-range ballistic missile
JWG	China-India Joint Working Group
LAC	Line of Actual Control
MIRV	multiple, independently targeted reentry vehicle
MPC&A	material protection, control, and accounting
MTCR	Missile Technology Control Regime
NATO	North Atlantic Treaty Organization
NDU	National Defense University
NPT	Non-Proliferation Treaty
NSG	Nuclear Suppliers Group
PLA	People's Liberation Army

SIIS	Shanghai Institute for International Studies
SLBM	submarine-launched ballistic missiles
SSBN	nuclear-powered ballistic missile submarine
START	Strategic Arms Reduction Treaty
WMD	weapons of mass destruction

1
Background

In May 1998, India and then Pakistan conducted a series of nuclear tests that took the world by surprise. Suddenly, the number of declared nuclear-weapon powers jumped from five to seven. International efforts to stop the spread of nuclear weapons, which had achieved gradual but substantial results since the end of the cold war, were clearly threatened. Indeed, the South Asian nuclear developments posed a severe challenge to the very concept of non-proliferation.

The crisis, however, does not necessarily portend further nuclear proliferation. Damage has been done to the non-proliferation regime, but it can—and should—be contained. As the nuclear situation in South Asia evolves, the international community must closely monitor the consequences of these nuclear blasts. China's response to the Indian and Pakistani explosions will have critical implications for the region. China is now at a crossroads: it has been actively involved in Pakistan's nuclear programs, but in recent years it has also joined most major nuclear control regimes. It is clearly in the interest of the international community to see China continue to follow and even to reinforce international nuclear non-proliferation norms.

This study examines China's reaction to the South Asian nuclear tests and suggests possible developments in its nuclear policy over the next five years. Many observers, both in China and in the United States, have suggested that China did not take India's nuclear tests seriously, arguing that since China's overall strength is so much greater than India's, China would not feel the need to take any measures to counter India's new nuclear-weapon capability.

In fact, assessing China's reaction to the South Asian nuclear tests is more complicated than this argumentation would suggest. Within the Chinese arms-control community, there have long been important differences between civilian policy makers and military strategists. The recent nuclear tests appear to have sharpened these differences, as the country's leaders debate China's response to the new perceived nuclear threat.

This study examines three scenarios for Chinese nuclear policy over the next five years. The first, and most likely, scenario is that China will maintain its current nuclear doctrine, modernization plans, and declared policy of non-proliferation. The second scenario is that China will expand its nuclear-weapon modernization plans and will undertake a moderate nuclear buildup, partly to counter an expected nuclear-weapon deployment by India. The third scenario—and the least likely one at present—is that China will reverse its commitments to international nuclear regimes if it comes to believe that its security is threatened by strategic developments in neighboring states. Whatever China decides will have important implications for the international community in general and for the United States in particular.

THE CURRENT STATE OF CHINESE NUCLEAR FORCES

Since exploding its first nuclear device in 1964, China has conducted forty-five nuclear tests. Its nuclear forces today include a triad of land-based missiles, bombers, and submarine-launched ballistic missiles, which collectively possess approximately 450 nuclear warheads. Land-based ballistic missiles remain the strongest element of today's Chinese nuclear arsenal (see Table 1).[1] China has about twenty DF-5 intercontinental ballistic missiles (ICBMs) with a striking range of 13,000 kilometers (8,100 miles).[2] It operates a single nuclear submarine (SSBN), the *Xia*, armed with 12 Julang-1 submarine-launched ballistic missiles (SLBMs) with a range of 1,700 kilometers (1,100 miles).

Within China's nuclear triad, its air force is the weakest element. The Chinese air force has more than 100 medium-range H-5 and H-6 bombers, some of which are nuclear-capable.[3] With a flying range of more than 3,000 kilometers (1,900 miles), the H-6 can reach all Asian countries, but its capability to penetrate air-defense systems is poor. The H-7, the first supersonic and only modern bomber in China, is being developed by the Xi'an Aircraft Company. This all-weather bomber will be capable of carrying out nuclear missions for the Chinese air force and navy.[4]

China's long-range and intermediate-range ballistic missiles (IRBMs) are perhaps more relevant to South Asia. In addition to the DF-5s, China has:

- at least 10 DF-4 land-based missiles with a striking range of 4,700 kilometers (3,000 miles)
- 38 DF-3 and DF-3A missiles with striking ranges of 2,650 and 2,800 kilometers (1,650 and 1,750 miles)
- 30 DF-21 and DF-21A missiles with striking ranges of 1,700 and 1,800 kilometers (1,080 and 1,120 miles), respectively.

China has exported short-range DF-11 (M-11) missiles to Pakistan. These have a striking range of 280 kilometers (175 miles) and are capable of carrying nuclear weapons.[5]

On the whole, the Chinese strategic nuclear force includes at least 20 ICBMs, 80 IRBMs, 120 nuclear-capable bombers, and 12 SLBMs.[6] This study will further elaborate the future of Chinese nuclear capabilities in Chapter 4.

In general, Chinese strategic nuclear forces and technologies have not made revolutionary advances but have evolved gradually since their establishment in the 1970s. The key area of improvement and growth has been the number and accuracy of medium- and short-range ballistic missiles. China now uses global-positioning satellite systems, for example, and provides warheads with terminal guidance packages to improve the accuracy of those missiles.[7] Although China did decide to sign the Comprehensive Test Ban Treaty (CTBT) in 1996, the 1998 nuclear tests in South Asia raise some concerns about whether it will continue to adhere to nuclear-weapon control regimes.

NUCLEAR DETERRENCE STRATEGY

Until the early 1980s, Chinese military strategy had been to prepare to "fight early, fight an all-out war, and fight a nuclear war." In 1985 the Chinese military leadership made a strategic turn, shifting from an emphasis on a possible World War III to preparing the Chinese military for limited warfare. At the same time, People's Liberation Army (PLA) analysts started to pay more attention to deterrence as a means of defense.

TABLE 1
China's Ballistic Missile Bases

Location	Brigades	Missiles	Targets
Shenyang, Liaoning Province	3	DF-3/DF-21	Northeast Asia
Huangshan, Anhui Province	2–3	DF-15	Taiwan
Kunming, Yunnan Province	2	DF-3/DF-21	Southeast Asia, India
Luoning, Henan Province	3	DF-4/DF-5	Russia, United States
Huaihua, Hunan Province	2	DF-4	Russia
Xining, Qinghai Province	3	DF-3/DF-4	Russia, India

Other possible sites:
Tonghua, Jilin; Xuanhua,
Hebei; Yidu, Shandong;
Wuzhai, Shanxi; Tongdao,
Hunan; Jianshui, Yunnan;
and various sites in Gansu.

Sources: "Nuclear Weapons and Sino-Indian Relations," *Southern Asia Policy Brief* (Washington, D.C.: Henry L. Stimson Center, June 15, 1998); Rodney W. Jones and Mark G. McDonough, *Tracking Nuclear Proliferation: A Guide in Maps and Charts, 1998* (Washington, D.C.: Carnegie Endowment for International Peace, 1998).

National Defense Theory, a PLA National Defense University book, is a unique and comprehensive elaboration of current nuclear thinking and a critical source for understanding China's deterrent strategy.[8] The military authors of this edited volume detail the history and current status of deterrence for China's national-security doctrine. They point out that while deterrence has played a prominent role in international strategic thinking since the end of World War II, its roots can actually be traced to military practices in ancient

Chinese times. Two thousand years ago, for example, Sun Zi advocated "overwhelming the enemy without fighting." This PLA book is extremely useful for clarifying aspects of Chinese military strategy and nuclear doctrine that heretofore have not been well understood.[9]

The authors of *National Defense Theory* identify the key Chinese features of deterrence as protecting the national interests and dispelling threats to the country. While in their view Chinese deterrence is limited to self-defense, other nations, particularly the United States, use deterrence as part of an offensive military strategy and reserve the right to the first use of nuclear weapons in any conflict.

In the Chinese authors' view, deterrence is a complex strategy, neither war nor peace, but something in between and existing on multiple levels. Deterrence can be divided into conventional deterrence, nuclear deterrence, outer-space deterrence, and so on. Conventional deterrence, in turn, can be both all-out, as in the use of conventional forces to deter a global war, or limited to a regional conflict. For an all-out or people's war, China would mobilize its massive population and resources to thwart the escalation of a conflict into a full-scale war. Regional deterrence would be used to oppose "hegemonic aggression" and expansion in China's neighboring areas. Limited nuclear deterrence would be used to oppose a possible nuclear war aimed at China. Such nuclear deterrence is viewed as a second-strike force that would retaliate against limited targets in the enemy country. Finally, China may develop a limited space-deterrence capability to compete in the military use of space with other powers.

As the above discussion shows, deterrence for these Chinese strategists can take both violent and nonviolent forms, involving the use of botn conventional weapons or even tactical nuclear weapons to deter a larger conflict. Thus, "violent deterrence" would involve the preparation and use of force to deter the outbreak of war or to stop the escalation and expansion of a war already started. "Nonviolent deterrence" includes the use of diplomacy, economics, science and technology, trade, and military aid to head off military and political tensions that could lead to war.[10]

During interviews conducted by this author in October 1998 in Beijing, a number of nuclear scientists and senior diplomats confirmed that China remains committed to maintaining sufficient nuclear forces to provide "limited nuclear deterrence." In other words, China will retain sufficient forces to launch a retaliatory strike after an adversary's nuclear attack. Officially, however, the Chinese leadership rarely acknowledges the role of nuclear deterrence. A national-defense adviser interviewed for this study, for example, said frankly that he should not answer any questions about Chinese nuclear doctrine, indicating how sensitive the issue remains in China today.

China's limited-war strategy and doctrine of limited deterrence have been in place for about a decade, during which China has not built a large nuclear force, rather a force focused on powerful, high-precision weapons with a high rate of survivability. The key question now is whether that doctrine will change as a consequence of the South Asian nuclear tests.

CURRENT CHINESE NUCLEAR POLICY

Chinese behavior toward nuclear-weapon control regimes has not been simple or straightforward. Several steps taken by the Chinese are generally regarded as positive developments. China joined the International Atomic Energy Agency (IAEA) in January 1984, signed the Nuclear Non-Proliferation Treaty (NPT) in March 1992, supported the indefinite extension of that treaty in May 1995, ceased nuclear testing and announced a unilateral moratorium on further testing in July 1996, signed the CTBT in September 1996, publicly announced a set of guidelines to govern nuclear-related exports in September 1997, officially joined the Zangger Committee (a coordinating body of nuclear-supplier nations that sets the standards for exporting nuclear fuel and equipment to non-nuclear-weapon states) in October 1997, and issued Regulations for Controlling the Export of Dual-Use Nuclear Goods and Relevant Technologies in June 1998.

But there have also been continuing concerns about Chinese practices, including the lack of an effective national export-control system to monitor transfers of nuclear, biological, chemical, missile, and dual-use exports; reports of Chinese noncompliance with its 1992 pledge to abide by the original 1987 Missile Technology Control Regime (MTCR) guidelines and its 1994 bilateral statement with the United States to accept the "inherent capability" concept[11] defining missiles associated with the MTCR; its refusal to adhere to the revised 1993 MTCR guidelines; and instances of nuclear-related exports and assistance to Pakistan.[12]

There is considerable evidence to support allegations of Chinese assistance to Pakistan's nuclear weapon program. In 1983, for example, U.S. intelligence reported that China had transferred a complete nuclear-weapon blueprint to Pakistan, along with weapons-grade uranium for two nuclear weapons. In 1986, China signed a nuclear-cooperation agreement with Pakistan, after which a number of Chinese scientists began assisting that country in the enrichment of weapons-grade uranium. China also provided Pakistan with nuclear products and technology, such as research and power reactors and information for uranium enrichment. In 1995, the China Nuclear Energy Industry Corporation exported about 5,000 ring magnets to a Pakistani nuclear laboratory that was not subject to IAEA inspections (and a suspected nuclear-weapons laboratory). In 1996, China reportedly sold to a Pakistani nuclear site a special industrial furnace and high-technology diagnostic equipment that could be used to construct nuclear bombs.[13]

As a nuclear power with worldwide influence, China has chosen to employ different policies toward nuclear-weapon and non-nuclear-weapon states. China regularly urges major nuclear powers such as the United States and Russia to abandon their nuclear-deterrence policies and to reduce substantially their nuclear-weapon stockpiles. China has also invited all nuclear-weapon states to commit themselves not to be the first to use such weapons at any time or under any circumstances. It has further called on all states that have deployed nuclear weapons outside their borders to retrieve them within national boundaries. China, Russia, and the United States have agreed not to target each other with strategic nuclear weapons.[14]

To non-nuclear states, China pledges unconditionally not to use or to threaten to use nuclear weapons. It supports efforts to establish nuclear-free zones, and has signed and approved the relevant protocols of a series of treaties for such measures in Latin America and the Caribbean, the South Pacific, and Africa. In 1995, China reiterated its commitment unconditionally to provide non-nuclear states and nuclear-weapon-free zones with negative security assurances, and for the first time promised to provide them with positive security assurances.[15]

As a general policy, China has advocated the complete prohibition and destruction of nuclear weapons and has opposed the development and deployment of outer-space weapons or missile-defense systems. China also supports an early conclusion of the Convention on Banning the Production of Fissile Materials for Nuclear Weapons or Other Nuclear Explosive Devices (also known as the Fissile Material Cut-off Treaty, or FMCT). In October 1994, the foreign ministers of China and the United States issued a joint statement on a multilateral and effectively verifiable FMCT. In April 1997, China and the other four declared nuclear-weapon states reiterated their call for the conclusion of an FMCT as soon as possible. China endorses the IAEA's Program for Strengthening the Effectiveness and Promoting the Efficiency of the Safeguard System.[16]

Against the debatable Chinese record of non-proliferation, the key question for strategists is what kind of impact the South Asian nuclear tests will have on China's nuclear doctrine and what Chinese nuclear policy will look like in five years. By 2005, a new nuclear-security pattern will fully emerge in South Asia, and China will react to it accordingly.

2
India's Nuclear Tests: Sino-Indian Mutual Concerns

SINO-INDIAN SECURITY RELATIONS, 1949–1998

For the decade following the establishment of the People's Republic of China in 1949, the Sino-Indian relationship was relatively stable. In 1954, the two governments declared the Five Principles of Peaceful Coexistence in the Agreement on Trade between India and the Tibet region of China. Jawaharlal Nehru, prime minister of India from 1947 to 1964, acknowledged that Tibet was an integral part of China, and the two governments adopted a friendly policy toward each other. In 1959, the Dalai Lama, the religious leader of Tibet, escaped from a Chinese military attack and fled to India. Since then, the Dalai Lama's use of India as a home base for campaigns against Chinese control in Tibet has remained a source of tension between the two countries.[17]

Territorial disputes are another irritant in Sino-Indian security relations. China rejects the so-called McMahon Line, drawn by the British in 1914 to separate China and India, as an unjust colonialist manipulation. In 1962, territorial frictions escalated into a two-month border war in which the neighbors fought along the eastern and western sectors of their Himalayan border. After pushing back Indian forces, China called for a cease-fire and offered to withdraw its forces twenty kilometers from the Line of Actual Control (LAC). This defeat of Indian troops by the Chinese army left continued tensions and distrust along the border, as each side still claims that territories rightfully belonging to it are occupied by the other.

In 1964, China exploded its first nuclear device. By the late 1950s and early 1960s, the Sino-Soviet alliance, established in 1950, had already been transformed into an antagonistic relationship, and Beijing was engaged in confrontation with both the Soviet Union and the United States. Although Mao Zedong called nuclear weapons a "paper tiger," China worried about possible nuclear strikes by either or both nuclear superpowers and began to develop its own nuclear arsenal in defense.[18]

Nevertheless, India saw these developments in a different light. That the Chinese development of a nuclear capability two years after the brief border war triggered India's own nuclear aspirations should not have been a surprise. Even before the Chinese test (and with some knowledge of the forthcoming Chinese breakthrough), some Indian officials had begun to voice India's need for acquiring nuclear weapons of its own. In public debates, arguments ranged from unconditional opposition to all nuclear weapons to the unequivocal pursuit of them. By the late 1960s, Indian nuclear opponents had lost ground to the emerging consensus in favor of the nuclear option. Among the reasons cited by India for its rejection of the Nuclear Non-Proliferation Treaty in 1968 was its concern with China's new status as a nuclear power.

India's first detonation of a nuclear device in Pokhran in 1974 enjoyed a high measure of public support. Still, it is worth noting that arguments for a non-nuclear-weapon policy continued not only from civilian officials, but also from military officials who warned that the costs of such a policy would exceed its actual benefits for Indian security. M. J. Desai, former secretary general of the Ministry of External Affairs, said that a nuclear race with China would retard India's economic and social programs, weaken the country internally, and eliminate its political influence in Asia and Africa.[19]

During the 1970s and 1980s, Sino-Indian relations continued to deteriorate. China aligned itself with Pakistan, while India lent support to Vietnam, China's rival. In 1979 and 1981, the Chinese and Indian foreign ministers exchanged visits and agreed to seek a negotiated solution to their boundary dispute. The two sides conducted eight rounds of talks between 1981 and 1987 but failed to find common ground. In 1986–1987, new territorial friction erupted during Indian military exercises and resulted in a fresh spate of accusations and warnings by both nations.

In 1988, Rajiv Gandhi, Indian prime minister, visited China, after which Sino-Indian relations began to improve. Both sides agreed to establish a China-India Joint Working Group to develop conditions for "a fair and reasonable settlement" and "to maintain peace and tranquility in the border region." Li Peng, the Chinese premier, visited India in 1991 and the two governments signed a series of agreements on diplomatic exchanges, border trade, and science and technology. Bilateral relations improved markedly after Narasimha Rao, the Indian prime minister, visited Beijing in 1993 and the two governments signed an Agreement on the Maintenance of Peace and Tranquility along the LAC.[20]

Security measures negotiated by the Joint Working Group include twice-yearly joint military meetings, the installation of military communication links at key points along both the eastern and western borders, mutual transparency on the location of military units along the LAC, prior notification of military maneuvers and troop movements along the border, and exchanges between high-level defense officials. The 1993 Agreement on the Maintenance of Peace and Tranquility contains the following key provisions:

- The two countries will resolve the border issue through peaceful and friendly consultations.
- The two sides will "strictly respect and observe" the LAC, pending an ultimate solution.
- The two sides agree to reduce their military forces along the LAC in conformity with the agreed requirements of the principle of mutual and equal security ceilings.
- The two sides will work out effective confidence-building measures (CBM) along the LAC.[21]

The high point of this period of relative Sino-Indian rapprochement was the historic visit by Chinese President Jiang Zemin to New Delhi in late 1996. The two sides signed the Agreement on CBM in the Military Field along the LAC, according to which their governments pledged:

- to limit the number of field-army troops, border-defense forces, paramilitary forces, and major categories of armaments along the LAC;
- to avoid holding large-scale military exercises near the LAC and to notify the other side of exercises involving one brigade group (that is, 5,000 troops);

- not to discharge firearms, cause biodegradation, use hazardous chemicals, set off explosives, or hunt with firearms within two kilometers of the LAC;
- to maintain and expand telecommunications links between border meeting points at designated places along the LAC.[22]

In light of the gradually improved Sino-Indian security relationship, observers might be puzzled to see the Indian nuclear tests justified by references to the "Chinese threat." India understands that China has been a nuclear-weapon state for more than three decades and that its potential nuclear threat to India has perhaps reduced with the gradual establishment of CBMs. The key question remains: Why did India decide to conduct nuclear tests in Pokhran again after twenty-four years of its non-nuclear weapon policy—and why now?

INDIA'S PERCEPTION OF THE NUCLEAR THREAT

Before conducting its first nuclear test in 1974, India's nuclear policy was directed toward the perceived threat from China. After Pakistan started its own nuclear program and Indo-Pakistani relations worsened during the 1970s and 1980s, however, ambiguity and uncertainty developed in Indian strategic thinking. By the mid-1980s, Indian strategists were convinced that Pakistan had developed an effective nuclear-weapon program; they subsequently viewed Pakistan as India's main nuclear threat. In the early 1990s, some observers argued that since India had lived under the Chinese nuclear shadow for more than twenty-five years, it surely could live with it for another twenty-five years under the improved bilateral relationship.[23]

It is worth noting again that the policy community in India remained divided on the question of China. Key officials of the Ministry of External Affairs were keen to improve ties with Beijing, while defense planners feared Chinese expansionist ambitions and kept a watchful eye on the areas across the LAC. Some military analysts also worried that a wealthy and newly powerful China would be dominated by nationalist ideas and argued that India should cooperate with other Asian nations to contain China.[24] Throughout this period, the issue of Tibet and the territorial disputes remained sources of tension between China and India.

In *Nuclear Weapons in Third World Context*, a 1981 Indian study of nuclear deterrence and the Indian strategic environment, several military and civilian analysts concluded that only nuclear weapons would deter a nuclear-armed aggressor. With respect to China, they believed, an India without nuclear weapons would suffer the same humiliating defeat as in 1962.[25] General Krishnaswami Sundarji, former chief of staff of the Indian army, wrote in 1995 that his country needed "both a nuclear and a conventional minimum capability to deter China and Pakistan," adding that, "if the Chinese use only tactical nuclear weapons, India would do likewise."[26]

Since the early 1980s, the annual reports of the Indian Ministry of Defense have persisted in identifying China as India's most formidable threat.[27] "China is potential threat number one," George Fernandes, defense minister, said in May 1998: "The potential threat from China is greater than that from Pakistan and any person who is concerned about India's security must agree with that." Answering questions about a supposed Chinese military buildup around India, Fernandes stated that, "China has its nuclear weapons stockpiled in Tibet along India's borders. I'm sure they are directed elsewhere also."[28] Fernandes's assertiveness likely has its roots in his personal history of anticommunism and antisocialism; he has passionately involved himself in prodemocracy movements in Tibet and Myanmar. For Fernandes, it is simply not in India's interests to understate its problems with China.[29]

One day after India's first round of nuclear tests in May 1998, Atal Bihari Vajpayee, prime minister of India, wrote to U.S. President Bill Clinton:

> I have been deeply concerned at the deteriorating security environment, especially the nuclear environment, faced by India for some years past. We have an overt nuclear weapon state on our borders, a state which committed armed aggression against India in 1962. Although our relations with that country have improved in the last decade or so, an atmosphere of distrust persists mainly due to the unresolved border problem. To add to the distrust that country has materially helped another neighbor of ours to become a covert nuclear weapons state. At the hands of this bitter neighbor we have suffered three aggressions in the last 50 years.[30]

Rajendrasinh Rana, chief of the State Bharatiya Janata Party (BJP), said that, "the tests were a befitting reply to our hostile neighbors."[31] But disagreements do exist among Indian policy makers. Inder Kumar Gujral, a former prime minister, advised Prime Minister Vajpayee not to project the nuclear tests as a BJP victory and warned against cultivating a chauvinist image of India. Gujral criticized Vajpayee's adventurism and lamented that his successor had encouraged the defense minister to take over India's foreign policy.[32]

Even the Indian army is wary of Fernandes's provocative comments on China. One general said that, "We simply cannot afford to antagonize the Chinese at this point. . . . We are fully stretched in combating insurgency in the country and if we have to deal with renewed tensions on the LAC, the army could well break down."[33]

Nevertheless, Fernandes may represent the "silent majority" on Sino-Indian security relations.[34] Although India has backed down from any confrontation with China for the moment, the most fundamental shift in the Vajpayee government strategy has been its reorientation away from Pakistan and toward China. It seems that New Delhi has concluded, again, that China is the real and long-term threat.[35]

India's internal debate on its policy toward China was carefully monitored by the Chinese, for whom words count—especially when uttered by Indian leaders. For those in India who wished to threaten China, the message was received clearly. Despite its restrained reaction, China was alarmed.

THE IMPACT OF INDIA'S NUCLEAR TESTS ON CHINA'S NATIONAL SECURITY

Two PLA senior colonels said in interviews that they were not surprised by India's nuclear tests because that country has simply shifted from being an undeclared to being a declared nuclear power. This tells exactly how well the Chinese are aware of the Indian nuclear program. Despite China's more mature nuclear development, India's looming nuclear potential has had a substantial impact on China's national security.

The controversy surrounding Tibet has caused repeated conflicts of national interest between China and India. *Xinhua*, the official Chinese news agency, commented that the Indian government tried in vain to obstruct China's liberation of Tibet but continues to provide the Dalai Lama a site to launch campaigns in support of Tibetan separatism. China perceived the Dalai Lama's endorsement of the Indian tests as "sinister relations between the Indian government and the Dalai clique." From the Chinese perspective, India has maintained an aggressive drive toward its northern boundary and has occupied some 90,000 square kilometers of Chinese territory since its independence from Britain. In October 1962, New Delhi continued to pursue what the Chinese called a policy of expansionism, which triggered an invasion of China. Citing the recently improved Sino-Indian relations, the *Xinhua* article stated that the "'China threat' advocated by the Vajpayee government is not a fact. But the interference from a group of Indian political figures with China's internal affairs is a matter of record."[36]

A second impact on China is India's historical determination to build up its nuclear power. One recent article in the PLA's *Liberation Army Daily* detailed Chinese perceptions of Indian nuclear developments, including a policy in existence since 1974 that reserves the option of building nuclear weapons for deterrence. China believes that India conducted nuclear research for weapons purposes and stored nuclear-weapon parts, which can be assembled as nuclear weapons when necessary. It "adopted the policy of vigorous development and comprehensive improvement." As a result, India today possesses nine nuclear-power plants, six heavy-water plants, seven nuclear-research reactors, four plutonium-reprocessing facilities, and three uranium-enrichment plants.[37]

The Chinese assessment of India's nuclear development is confirmed by Indian sources, who note that, "A nuclear bomb program is technically feasible, politically highly desirable, strategically inescapable and economically not only sustainable but actually advantageous. . . . India's nuclear program has always been strongly influenced by the China factor."[38] *Xinhua* claimed that India's 1998–1999 defense budget increased by more than 14 percent from the previous year's $9.38 billion to $10.70 billion.[39]

Thirdly, China is aware of India's potential to target it with nuclear weapons, and it keeps a watchful eye on the development of Indian nuclear doctrine. A senior Chinese official in Beijing said that, "from mutual confidence we have now moved to mutual apprehension."[40]

In August 1998, Indian Prime Minister Vajpayee spoke to the Lok Sabha (the lower house of parliament) about the government's nuclear policy. He made the commitment not to use nuclear weapons first, announced a moratorium on further underground nuclear tests, and accepted the basic concept of a test ban. Thus, while India has declared itself to be a de facto nuclear-weapon power, its nuclear-weapon policy and doctrine remain unclear. Whether India decides to sign the CTBT is a question that will have a strong effect on China's national security.[41]

In December 1998, Indian Prime Minister Vajpayee declared that his country would "maintain the deployment of a deterrent which is both minimum and credible," marking his first public statement that India may have already deployed nuclear weapons.[42] A Chinese senior colonel also claimed recently that India has provided its army with Agni missiles with a maximum range of 2,500 kilometers (1,550 miles).[43]

Fourth, the Indo-Pakistan relationship also worries China. In 1947, the two countries declared independence from Britain and immediately fought their first war over the disputed territory of Kashmir. In 1965, India and Pakistan fought a second war. In 1971, their third war, fought in what was then East Pakistan, resulted in the defeat of Pakistan and the creation of Bangladesh as an independent country. Responding to India's 1974 nuclear test, Zulfiqar Ali Bhutto, Pakistani prime minister, vowed that his country would "eat grass" if necessary to achieve a nuclear force. Since the early 1980s, the so-called Indian-Pakistani cold war has acquired a nuclear dimension. In 1994, Nawaz Sharif (the then-former and now current prime minister) announced that Pakistan had an atomic bomb. In 1996, India tested the Prithvi missile, which is capable of carrying nuclear weapons and which Pakistani officials believed was developed to attack their cities.[44] Pakistan tested the Ghauri missile, with a range of 1,500 kilometers (930 miles), in April 1998.

Many experts agree that deploying nuclear weapons could put India and Pakistan in a dangerous standoff. One Western diplomat based in Islamabad noted that it would take only about three minutes for nuclear-armed missiles to fly from launch sites near the two countries' border to each other's capitals. "There is no reaction time here. . . . We are eyeball to eyeball," Gohar Ayub Khan, Pakistani foreign minister, told the *Washington Post*.[45] Pakistan reportedly expected an air strike by India and Israel on the eve of its first nuclear tests in late May 1998, alarming the U.S. and Chinese governments about a possible war in South Asia.[46]

While China has assisted Pakistan's nuclear development and has provided short-range missiles to that country, a nuclear standoff between Pakistan and India and the proliferation of nuclear weapons among Islamic countries are not necessarily China's goals. The nuclear tests by the two South Asian countries perhaps have finally exposed the impact of nuclear proliferation on China's national security. Islamic independence movements within northwest China threaten its own internal stability, while a nuclear conflict between Pakistan and India would impact China's border regions. Zhang Yishan, permanent representative of the Chinese delegation to the UN CTBT Preparatory Committee in Vienna, said that, "We would like to once again solemnly urge India and Pakistan to exercise their greatest restraint, to stop all nuclear tests, to discard plans to develop nuclear weapons, and not to deploy nuclear weapons."[47]

This leads to the final Chinese concern—India's reluctance to follow China in signing the CTBT. In August 1996, India decided not to sign the CTBT, but to keep its nuclear-weapon option open.[48] The 1998 tests conducted by India and its continuing refusal to sign the CTBT create, in Chinese eyes, new threats to China's southern border security.[49]

3
Chinese Reactions to the Indian and Pakistani Tests

CHINA'S INTERNAL DEBATE ON NON-PROLIFERATION ISSUES AND POLICY

Arms control is a relatively new subject in China. As one Chinese diplomat explained to this author in Beijing in October 1998, China is just beginning to learn that international-security regimes can both favor and constrain Chinese interests. He said that China needs to improve its arms-control institutions and to deepen its understanding of how international arms-control mechanisms work.

There are four categories of arms-control institutes in China (see Table 2). In descending order of policy relevance, these are the Ministry of Foreign Affairs, the People's Liberation Army (PLA), government research institutes, and their civilian counterparts. Among them, the Ministry of Foreign Affairs and the PLA are the two most important institutional decision makers on international-security issues. The key agency within the ministry is the Department of Arms Control, equivalent to the U.S. Arms Control and Disarmament Agency. The PLA maintains a number of arms-control-related institutes, including:

- the China Institute for International Strategic Studies (CIISS), affiliated with the Second Department of the General Staff Department (GSD)
- the Commission of Science, Technology, and Industry for National Defense (COSTIND), under military and civilian lead-

ership until early 1998 and now an entirely civilian organization. COSTIND also includes several affiliated institutes, such as the Chinese Academy of Engineering Physics and the Institute of Applied Physics and Computational Mathematics (IAPCM), both of which offer strong scientific and technological research and development capabilities
- the National Defense University's (NDU) Institute for Strategic Studies
- the Academy of Military Science (AMS)
- the China Defense Science and Technology Information Center (CDSTIC).

In addition, there are several organizations managed or supported by retired PLA officers in Beijing, such as the Foundation of International Strategic Studies and the China Society for Strategy and Management.

Government research centers constitute the third category of arms-control institutes. Among them, the China Institute of Contemporary International Relations (CICIR) is perhaps the most important. One senior fellow at CICIR said that his institute was the first in Beijing to conduct a comprehensive analysis of India's nuclear tests, after which staff members from other organizations came to CICIR to discuss its findings.[50] The Shanghai Institute for International Studies (SIIS) is another government research arm. The China Institute for International Studies (CIIS) in Beijing is a research institute for the Ministry of Foreign Affairs. CIIS staff members include scholars, politicians, and former ambassadors. In late 1998, the Chinese Academy of Social Sciences (CASS) proposed to establish a center for arms control that would serve the needs of both government and academic researchers.

Academic research institutes for arms control remain a new and limited phenomenon, but they may develop rapidly in the future due to their rich personnel resources and active international contacts. In 1991, the Program on Arms Control and Regional Security at Fudan University's Center for American Studies in Shanghai became the first nonofficial arms-control institute. Faculty members at Beijing University have also conducted arms control research.

The arms-control community in China includes a small number of influential figures whose expertise and reputations enhance the

TABLE 2
The Hierarchy of China's Arms Control Community

Ministry of Foreign Affairs
Department of Arms Control

People's Liberation Army
China Institute of International Strategic Studies (CIISS)
Commission of Science, Technology, and Industry for National
　Defense (COSTIND) [until early 1998]
Chinese Academy of Engineering Physics [until early 1998]
Institute of Applied Physics and Computational Mathematics
　(IAPCM) [until early 1998]
National Defense University Institute of Strategic Studies
　(NDU)
China Defense Science and Technology Information Center
　(CDSTIC)
Several organizations founded by retired PLA officers

Government Research Institutes
China Institute of Contemporary International Relations (CICIR)
China Institute of International Studies (CIIS)
Chinese Academy of Social Sciences (CASS)
Shanghai Institute of International Studies (SIIS)

↑　↓

Civilian Organizations
Program on Arms Control and Regional Security at Fudan
　University
Beijing University, faculty researchers
Other private organizations, including some in development

Source: author's compilation.

stature of the institutions in which they work. Among them are Sha Zukang at the Department of Arms Control of the Ministry of Foreign Affairs, Qian Shaojun and Lu Min at the old COSTIND, and Hu Side, Song Jiashu, and Chen Xueyin at the Chinese Academy of Engineering Physics.

The development and implementation of Chinese arms-control policy, including such major decisions as signing the NPT and CTBT, appear to be top-down processes, although bottom-up feedback tends to play an increasingly important role. Unlike the United States and Russia, whose presidents generally take the lead in international arms-control and disarmament negotiations, China delegates this responsibility to the Ministry of Foreign Affairs. Also unlike other countries, China sends diplomatic delegates instead of military advisers to the Geneva Conference on Disarmament. In 1993, a Chinese delegation, headed by a Ministry of Foreign Affairs official and including personnel from the Ministries of Chemical Industry, Public Health, National Defense, plus the GSD, signed the Chemical Weapons Convention. In 1996, China signed the CTBT after the Ministry of Foreign Affairs, joined by COSTIND and other departments, initiated the negotiation.

When the Ministry of Foreign Affairs faces a new mission in international-security negotiations, it functions like a central organ, assigning various tasks to arms-control-related institutes across the country. As some experts point out, however, the MFA traditionally lacks broad and in-depth technical expertise and thus seeks to resolve complicated issues through general political and diplomatic principles. In an interview in Beijing in October 1998, one Chinese diplomat acknowledged that the Ministry of Foreign Affairs focuses more on politics and diplomacy, but predicted that as China puts more efforts into arms control, there will be greater collaboration between the ministry and the PLA.

The PLA is a critical player in China's defense decision making and its role deserves more attention than it currently receives, particularly because it appears that in the future, Chinese nuclear policy will increasingly be defined by the military.

The PLA has both interest in and professional knowledge of arms control and disarmament and, consequently, exercises a substantial influence on the Ministry of Foreign Affairs and on China's decision-making process as a whole. Among all the institutes directly or indirectly involved in work related to the CTBT, the PLA's influence can be detected in both its resistance to and its endorsement of international-security regimes. In 1996, as the ministry was moving toward an endorsement of the CTBT, the PLA provided technical evidence that it claimed showed that the treaty was not in China's security interests. At the time, COSTIND successfully lobbied the ministry to accommodate some of the PLA's concerns.

The PLA was more reluctant than the Ministry of Foreign Affairs to accept both the NPT and the CTBT. Many military officers were concerned about the possible economic and strategic disadvantages if China joined the test ban. As a PLA senior colonel explained, China's military in 1996 still needed additional tests to improve the capability and safety of its nuclear-weapon stockpile.

In general, the PLA has been suspicious of multilateral security initiatives and resistant to calls for transparency in Chinese military budgets, doctrine, force structure, and relations with other nations. Members of the military-industrial sector, for example, were not happy with the suspension of arrangements to assist Iran with its nuclear energy program.[51] Whereas the Ministry of Foreign Affairs advocates international security regimes, the PLA views the ministry as weak on national security issues.[52]

The PLA's attitudes may have received support from former top military leaders such as Liu Huaqing, Zhang Zhen, and incumbent top officers Zhang Wannian and Chi Haotian. Liu, a former member of the Chinese Communist Party Standing Committee of the Political Bureau and vice chairman of the Central Military Commission (1992–1997), had long urged construction of a modernized and high-tech army. Liu repeatedly pointed out that the world's rapid economic development had resulted in a new form of competition in the military field, marked mainly by the building of quality armies with high technology. He stressed that the national defense industry was, in effect, a high-technology industry that concerned itself with national security and reflected comprehensive national strength.[53]

It would not be correct, however, to suggest that China's arms control decision-making process lacks central management or that the PLA has always opposed arms control negotiations. One military researcher suggested that the PLA did not want to publicize its disputes with the Ministry of Foreign Affairs and other civilian sectors. Instead, the PLA has sought consensus and active participation in international-security regimes. One Chinese diplomat echoed the view that the PLA could not oppose the process of arms control because the final decision came from the political leadership above both the ministry and the military. He said that a central task group coordinates all arms-control activities and submits all suggestions to top leaders for decision.[54]

In 1992, according to one interviewee, COSTIND played an important role in pushing China to sign the NPT. Later, a task team at COSTIND, headed by General Qian Shaojun, joined the second-round negotiations on the CTBT. Finally, in 1996, after negotiations initiated by the Ministry of Foreign Affairs and joined by COSTIND and other ministries, China signed the CTBT.

COSTIND enjoyed high prestige in China's defense planning and foreign-policy decision making. Tightly controlled by the Central Military Commission until early 1998, COSTIND perhaps played the most important role in Chinese deliberations on the CTBT at the technical level. Evidence indicates that the PLA still retains this central role. Recent developments seem to suggest that the PLA has won strong support from President Jiang Zemin. Other top leaders endorse the PLA's desire to establish a high-tech military force.

Together with COSTIND, other military institutes have also participated in China's arms-control decision making. The Second Department of the GSD is a key source of strategic analysis on national security and defense intelligence. It produces a daily report of major military events, which is circulated to the Central Military Commission, Political Bureau members, and heads of the PLA general departments.[55] The CIISS, directed by the Second Department, conducts research for the Ministries of Foreign Affairs and National Defense and for the GSD. Among other issues, it has undertaken negotiations on the MTCR and border demarcations. In 1992, staff members from the CIISS joined the U.S.-China-Britain nuclear export discussions.

The National Defense University and the Academy of Military Science engage in strategic and operational analysis, and report to the Central Military Commission and the GSD. Despite their limited functions, the two institutes have high military status and are headed by officers at the rank of general. In recent years, personnel from both institutes have been assigned to arms-control research and international activities.

As an entire functional system, the Second Department of the GSD, with its CIISS, NDU, AMS, and COSTIND institutes, collaborates in informing the top leadership and providing technical and policy options. The AMS sometimes coordinates and channels the submission of reports from these institutes to the General Office of the Central Military Commission, which then evaluates and summarizes them for the top leaders of the Standing Committee of the Political Bureau.[56] It is clear that both civilian and military officials play important roles in Chinese nuclear policy. While the two often disagree, final decisions always come from the top leadership, which is often a small leading group.

THE OFFICIAL GOVERNMENT REACTION

After India's first round of nuclear tests on May 11, 1998, China's immediate reaction was silence. Within an hour of the morning announcement by New Delhi that the three nuclear tests had occurred, *Xinhua* reported this news without further comment. On May 12, Zhu Bangzao, spokesman for the Ministry of Foreign Affairs, did not reply when asked if China would resume its nuclear tests as a result of the Indian tests. *China Daily*, China's official English newspaper, published a brief story on the blast, and *Renmin Ribao*, the Chinese-language People's Daily, had a small news item on page 6. The newspapers did not offer additional comments of their own, but reported that the United States had condemned the blasts.[57]

There were good reasons for this initial silence. First, China has always claimed that respect for the sovereignty of other countries and a policy of noninterference in their internal affairs are major principles of its international relations—and it has criticized other countries for not adhering to these same principles. China clearly remembers the criticism it received after its 1964 nuclear tests. Second, China, like the United States and other countries, was surprised by the Indian nuclear tests and needed time to prepare an appropriate response. Third, the initial silence may also have indicated a lack of consensus among Chinese political and military leaders, for whom non-proliferation is a relatively new and highly sensitive issue.

Two days after the Indian tests, however, China joined in the criticism expressed by many other countries. Zhu Bangzao stated that, "the Chinese government expresses grave concern over India's nuclear tests. . . . India's nuclear tests under such circumstances run counter to the international trend and are not in the interest of South Asia's peace and stability."[58] In the wake of India's second round of nuclear tests on May 13, China reacted immediately. The Ministry of Foreign Affairs stated that, "The Chinese government is deeply shocked by this and hereby expresses its strong condemnation. . . . The Indian government, which itself has undermined the international effort in banning nuclear tests so as to obtain the hegemony in South Asia in defiance of the world opinion, has even maliciously accused China of posing a nuclear threat to India. This is utterly groundless. . . . This gratuitous accusation by India against China is solely for the purpose of finding excuses for the development of its nuclear weapons."[59]

Qian Qichen, Chinese vice premier, pointed out that a nuclear arms race is likely to take place in South Asia if India's nuclear testing is not stopped.[60] On June 3, a senior Chinese foreign affairs official said that, "I don't want to frighten anyone, but no one likes being anyone else's target. . . . We don't want to be and are not India's enemy, but at least we have to think twice." He added that China could not rule out the possibility of resuming nuclear tests if the situation in South Asia worsened.[61] Despite the official's opening disclaimer, his remarks did indeed frighten a number of other countries about China's nuclear intentions.

Then, in a 45-minute interview with Jean Miot, chairman of Agence France-Presse, Chinese President Jiang Zemin made the following assertions:

- Although China possesses nuclear weapons, it has made a unilateral pledge to use such weapons only in response to a nuclear attack;
- China favors the complete prohibition of nuclear tests and has no intention of restarting such tests of its own;
- India makes China a potential target of its nuclear weapons and must be blamed for the new tensions in South Asia.[62]

During an early-July 1998 visit to Central Asia, Jiang reiterated that China supports the CTBT and opposes nuclear proliferation in any form. "The current tension in South Asia," he said, "was triggered by India single-handedly."[63] When India proposed to sign a pact promising no first use of nuclear weapons with China, Tang Guoqiang, a foreign-ministry spokesman, said that India should first abandon its nuclear-weapon programs and sign the CTBT and the NPT immediately and unconditionally.[64] *Xinhua* reported Indian assertions that it would not sign the CTBT under what it calls the dictates of nuclear powers and would not succumb to any external pressure to postpone or cancel its nuclear-weapon or missile programs.[65]

Interestingly, Beijing did not attribute the Indian nuclear tests solely to New Delhi's perception of a threat from China. *Xinhua* noted that the Indian BJP government attempted to use the nuclear tests to divert people's attention from its inability to tackle domestic problems: the bomb had become a handy tool to consolidate the cohesion of the coalition government.[66] A *Xinhua* article made the following analysis: "India has always harbored ambitions of becoming a major power.... After 50 years of development, however, India has not extricated itself from its status as a poor country, and average output per capita is far down in world rankings. India has been demanding for a long time to become a permanent member of the UN Security Council, and to achieve an international status commensurate with having the second highest population in the world." Thus, in China's view, India wished to achieve great power status by acquiring nuclear weapons, which was clearly revealed by India's attempt to use its nuclear status to this end during Indian-U.S. talks after the tests.[67]

Moreover, the Chinese government has tried to balance outright condemnation with insistence that the Indian government maintain stable relations with China. After India and Pakistan conducted nuclear tests, Tang Jiaxuan, Chinese minister of foreign affairs, vowed that, "We have no intention of imposing sanctions" on the two countries. "As an integrated stance of Chinese foreign policy, we cannot approve countries' imposing sanctions at any time on any countries."[68]

Beijing urged New Delhi to respect the overall interests of the bilateral relationship and immediately to stop all statements and actions against China.[69] Speaking at a seminar in New Delhi, Zhou Gang, Chinese ambassador to India, called India's claim of a Chinese threat to India's security baseless. "The Chinese side could not but refute some wanton attack and accusation against China by certain personages in India in order to safeguard the friendly relations between our two countries and bring the Sino-Indian relations back onto the track."[70]

Beijing also closely watched the change in Indian leaders' attitudes. Chinese media often quoted Indian leaders whose comments appeared consistent with China's own policy positions. According to *Xinhua*, Indian Prime Minister Vajpayee conceded that there was peace, tranquility, and stability along the Sino-Indian border, and added that his government was eager to resolve the border dispute with China through dialogue.[71] In late July 1998, China Radio International reported that Indian Defense Minister Fernandes stressed the need to normalize Sino-Indian relations and for the two countries to remain friends. The Radio commented that this was his first statement on normalization of relations with China at least since May, when he made many anti-China statements.[72] In early August, *Xinhua* reported that Prime Minister Vajpayee, in a speech to the Lok Sabha, appealed to parliament to resolve border issues with China. He said that his government had never identified China as India's "biggest enemy," according to *Xinhua*.[73]

In general, the Chinese government has attempted a balanced, two-pronged approach to its relationship with India. In late July, during a meeting with an Indian official at the Regional Forum of the Association of South East Asian Nations (ASEAN), Chinese Foreign Minister Tang said that India had flagrantly run counter to the world non-proliferation trend. Tang hoped that India would abandon its nuclear-weapon programs, sign the CTBT, join the NPT, and improve Sino-Indian relations.[74]

THE PLA REACTION

These policy statements by the Chinese government do not reflect a final determination, but, at best, a tentative response to India's nuclear tests. Inside the government, debate continues. Indeed, the PLA's reaction to the tests has been much harsher than that of the Chinese government. One *Liberation Army Daily* article in May, for example, noted that, "India was too impatient to declare that, when necessary, it would not hesitate to use nuclear weapons" in international conflicts. India's nuclear tests had undermined "the security pattern and political atmosphere" in South Asia and its dream of being a regional hegemon is a "nightmare" for the world. The article warned that India will "eventually pick up a stone to drop it on its own feet."[75]

Another *Liberation Army Daily* article by Liu Yang and Guo Feng conveyed a sense of how PLA analysts view the Indian military. With an armed force of 1.36 million men (plus 700,000 paramilitary troops and a 2.8 million-man reserve), the Indian military ranks fourth in the world. (It is more than double that of the rest of South Asian countries combined.) Recent upgrades of its military equipment include air-force purchases of Russian Su-30 fighters and the navy's acquisition of Russian Kilo-class submarines.

India's military strategy, Liu and Guo argue, is "to seek hegemony in South Asia, contain China, control the Indian Ocean, and strive to become a military power in the contemporary world." They acknowledge that India has taken a defensive posture against China to maintain its military superiority in the Sino-Indian boundary region, but conclude ominously that because of India's development of Agni intermediate-range, nuclear-armed missiles, "China's central and south regions are within its range."[76]

In a similar assessment, four analysts from the China Defense Science and Technology Information Center claimed that India produced 350–475 kilograms of weapons-grade plutonium from 1960 to 1994 and that it possessed 245–370 kilograms by late 1994. Assuming 8 kilograms per nuclear device, the Chinese analysts concluded that the material could have been used for 30–46 nuclear weapons. The analysts also estimated that India would have 358–546 kilograms of weapons-grade plutonium—enough for 44–68 nuclear devices— by the end of 2000, and that India could produce about 8 kilograms per year of weapons-grade uranium, for use in the initial stage of thermonuclear-weapons (that is, hydrogen-bombs) development. India's delivery systems, according to the analysts, include the Prithvi I, II, and III ballistic missiles, which have payloads of 1,000, 500, and 500 kilograms, and striking ranges of 150, 250, and 350 kilometers (95, 155, and 220 miles), respectively. Posing a more direct threat to China are Agni I and II ballistic missiles, each with a 1,000-kilogram payload and striking ranges of 1,500 and 2,500 kilometers (950 and 1,550 miles), respectively. Finally, the analysts noted that India is developing an ICBM with a range of about 8,000 kilometers (5,000 miles).[77]

Senior Colonel Yang Haisheng, former deputy diplomatic military attaché to the Chinese Diplomatic Military Attaché's office in India, wrote that India has a budget for war with China and that its armed forces frequently conducted exercises aimed at China in the boundary region. He noted that India had exercised nuclear blackmail on Pakistan and had threatened China with its nuclear capabilities. Yang warned that if the international community turned a blind eye to India's behavior, "the evildoer" will continue to trouble the world.[78]

Chi Haotian, Chinese defense minister, said that the tense situation in South Asia was caused by the regional nuclear-arms race and that the "China threat" was just a rumor. The Chinese government was anxious and worried about the South Asian situation, he asserted, urging the countries involved to restrain themselves and to abandon immediately their nuclear weapon programs.[79]

Xiong Guangkai, deputy chief of the PLA General Staff, said on May 21 that, "New Delhi should pay more attention to feeding its poor than building nuclear weapons." Sources believed that PLA pressure was the reason for the harsher Chinese reaction to India's second round of nuclear tests. The PLA was perhaps worried about India's move to develop sophisticated tactical nuclear weapons.[80]

The initial silence after India's first round of nuclear tests, followed by inconsistent statements from senior diplomatic officials, probably indicates a lack of consensus among Chinese political and military leaders. Whereas the government wants to compromise, the PLA continues to express a more hard-line policy toward India.

CHINA'S REACTION TO THE PAKISTANI NUCLEAR TESTS

After India conducted five nuclear tests, Gohar Ayub Khan, foreign minister of Pakistan, said that, "It's a matter of when, not if, Pakistan will test."[81] On May 28, 1998, Pakistan announced that it had conducted five underground nuclear tests. Prime Minister Nawaz Sharif said that India's tests had changed the strategic balance and deterrence between the two countries. In a later address to reporters, Sharif said that, "Our security, and the peace and stability of the entire region, was gravely threatened. As any self-respecting nation, we had no choice left for us. Our hand was forced by the present Indian leadership's reckless actions. . . . We could not ignore the magnitude of the threat. . . . Today, the flames of the nuclear fire are all over. . . . I am thankful to God that . . . we have jumped into the flames . . . with courage."[82]

The tests were carried out at the Chagai Hills test site in Western Pakistan. The U.S. Geological Survey in Golden, Colorado, reported that the strongest test had a preliminary magnitude of 4.9 on the Richter scale, compared with the 5.4 measure of India's strongest blast. Sharif suggested that Pakistan might resort to nuclear weapons to prevent a defeat in either a nuclear or a conventional war. A Pakistani government statement announced that Pakistan's "long-range Ghauri missile is already being capped with nuclear warheads to give a befitting reply to any misadventure by the enemy." The missile has a range of 1,500 kilometers (930 miles), which means it can reach most of India's major cities.[83] A week before Pakistan's nuclear tests, L. K. Advani, Indian home minister, warned that India's nuclear tests had "brought about a qualitatively new stage in Indo-Pakistan relations" and that Pakistan should "roll back its anti-India policy, especially with regard to Kashmir."[84] Pakistan responded to India's threat with five nuclear tests of its own, and on May 30, Pakistan exploded one more nuclear device.[85]

During the weeks between the Indian and Pakistani nuclear tests, Islamabad and Beijing held security consultations. Some analysts hoped that China would offer Pakistan a nuclear defense assurance to deter it from going nuclear.[86] On May 18, Shamshad Ahmad, Pakistani foreign secretary, held talks with Chinese foreign ministry officials in Beijing. Radio Pakistan Network said that, "Pakistan wanted to take China, a time-tested friend, into confidence about the measures which need to be taken to safeguard national security."[87] At the same time, China's *Xinhua* quoted Pakistani Prime Minister Sharif as saying Pakistan would "not sit back" in the face of India's new threat.[88] When Ahmad returned home, *Xinhua* reported that, "he is fully satisfied with" the visit. According to *Xinhua*, the two sides exchanged views on the "severe impact on global non-proliferation efforts and the dangers posed" by India's nuclear tests. Ahmad said that, "the Chinese leadership has once again affirmed that the China-Pakistan relationship is an all-weather one which has stood the test of time."[89]

Apparently, however, China did not offer nuclear guarantees to Pakistan. Ahmad only told the public that China would not impose economic sanctions if Pakistan conducted its own nuclear tests.[90] (As mentioned above, China did not impose economic sanctions on India either.)

When Pakistan conducted its first nuclear tests, Zhu Bangzao, Chinese foreign ministry spokesman, said that China expressed its "deep regret" over Pakistan's action. He added that, "The Chinese government is deeply worried and disturbed about the nuclear arms race that has appeared in South Asia. We solemnly appeal to relevant countries in South Asia to exercise their maximum restraint, and immediately renounce their nuclear arms development plans so as to prevent the situation from further worsening and for the sake of peace and stability in South Asia."[91] Explaining China's reaction, a Chinese expert on South Asia said, "We knew there was a great possibility that Pakistan would follow [India's tests] because of the internal pressure its leaders face. But this is a rather difficult situation for China. We have a friendship with Pakistan, but we also have a strong stance against nuclear proliferation."[92]

It was also reported that, at the behest of U.S. President Clinton, Chinese President Jiang wrote to the Pakistani government urging it not to conduct a nuclear test just a few days before the blasts, an apparent sign of China's readiness to end its longstanding tie with Pakistan's nuclear program.[93] But, as Zhu Bangzao stated, "The present situation in South Asia was caused solely by India, while Pakistan's nuclear tests were conducted as reactions to India's 'intimidation.'"[94] There was no sign that the Sino-Pakistani relationship had degraded since Pakistan's nuclear tests. In late August, General Zhang Wannian, vice chairman of the Central Military Commission, received visiting General Jehangir Karamat, chairman of the Pakistani Joint Chiefs of Staff Committee and Chief of the Army Staff. Zhang noted that the two countries were friendly neighbors and that their relations have progressed smoothly over time. The two sides exchanged views on broad issues, and Zhang expressed his hope that frequent high-level visits would bring new life into the development of bilateral cooperation.[95] The meeting highlighted the difference between Sino-Pakistani relations and Sino-Indian relations, with the former featuring high-level strategic consultations altogether missing in the latter.

4

Three Scenarios for China's Nuclear Doctrine and Non-Proliferation Policy

How will China's nuclear doctrine and non-proliferation policy develop between now and the year 2005? This chapter will consider three scenarios.

MAINTENANCE OF THE STATUS QUO

A major policy shift by a great power generally occurs only after some dramatic event or series of events. The Indian nuclear tests of 1998 were such an event in the minds of China's foreign-policy leaders, who were particularly disturbed because India appeared to treat China as its primary threat. Yet both governments have tried to prevent a free fall in their relationship, and an actual nuclear confrontation between India and China in the near future remains highly unlikely. China will have at least five years to monitor the development of India's nuclear forces and to assess any possible nuclear threat to China. Until a new nuclear security pattern fully emerges in South Asia, China will most likely maintain its current nuclear policies and its current modernization plan, including the development and deployment of new DF-31 and DF-41 missiles.

India remains a poor country, Chinese analysts believe, and its nuclear programs will continue to be restrained by limited budgets. And while China is concerned about the Indian nuclear tests, it is also inured to the nuclear threat after having lived with the existence of Soviet and American nuclear warheads for years.[96]

Chinese scientists also have doubts about India's declared nuclear capabilities. They detected the three low-yield (200, 300, and 500 ton) tests, but questioned whether India's nuclear devices have been developed into usable weapons. Because the international seismic monitoring network did not even record the declared tests on May 13, Chinese scientists suspected that the declared yield of 500 tons of TNT was actually less than 50 tons. Chinese scientists were uncertain why India exaggerated its nuclear capabilities or whether it would conduct more tests. One analysis made by Chinese scientists was that the Indian tests attempted to perfect two designs: one for an enhanced atomic bomb, using various boosters to increase the yield of the plutonium core; the other for a thermonuclear device with many times the yield of a simple atomic bomb. Based on the available data, it seems that, despite Indian claims of success, they did not succeed in igniting a thermonuclear reaction.[97]

Another analyst suggested that China should pursue an independent foreign policy and exchange views with India. He argued that the South Asian nuclear tests have speeded up the transition to a multipolar world. According to his analysis, a nuclear balance between Pakistan and India is perhaps favorable to China's security interests. He encouraged the Chinese government to learn to live with another nuclear neighbor and to use the opportunity to stabilize relations with the South Asian nations.[98]

No Major Changes in the Development of Nuclear Doctrine and Forces

China's National Defense, a white paper issued by the Information Office of the State Council in July 1998, two months after India's nuclear tests, is perhaps the best official exposition of China's nuclear doctrine and non-proliferation policy. The white paper stated that, "India flagrantly carried out nuclear tests," that Pakistan then followed suit, and that these nuclear tests have "produced grave consequences on peace and stability in the South Asian region and the rest of the world."[99]

In general, however, the white paper assessed the international-security situation by stating that, "peace and development are the major themes of the present era. . . . The present international-security situation has continued to tend toward relaxation." China's fundamental task, the white paper continued, is to conduct economic construction, while national defense should remain "subordinate to and in the service of the nation's overall economic construction." A key element of China's defense policy is "active defense," that is, "striking only after the enemy has struck." According to the white paper, "China possesses a small number of nuclear weapons, entirely for meeting the needs of self-defense."[100]

The white paper appears to be consistent with China's defense policy since the late 1970s, when China started its modernization drive. The Chinese leadership has been clearly aware of economic constraints on China's defense development. In the 1980s, Deng Xiaoping urged the PLA to "exercise patience," and in the mid-1990s, Jiang Zemin warned against a large military budget. Commenting on the military-development strategy elaborated in the white paper, Chi Haotian, the defense minister, said that, "We should not blindly worship advanced weaponry. Rather, we should try to defeat a better-equipped enemy with whatever equipment we have at the moment."[101] It is likely, therefore, that China will maintain its current level of nuclear forces and will continue to adhere to its policy of no first use of nuclear weapons and no use or threat of using nuclear weapons against non-nuclear-weapon countries or zones. China will also, under this scenario, continue to observe the CTBT, NPT, and other nuclear regimes.

As part of the current national strategy, China will continue its nuclear-weapons modernization (see Table 3). It is estimated that China's stockpile contains more than 3 tons of weapons-grade, highly enriched uranium and 1 ton of separated plutonium, with which China can make an additional 200 nuclear weapons.[102]

In July 1998, one news account claimed that China had produced eight more DF-5 Mod 2 ICBMs.[103] If that number is confirmed, China will deploy at least 28 ICBMs by the year 2000. At the same time, China continued to test the DF-31 missile in 1998 as part of its strategic-weapons modernization effort.[104] The DF-31 is powered with solid-fuel propulsion and has a range of 8,000 kilometers (5,000 miles). First tested in 1995, the DF-31 may be deployed in the year 2000 armed with multiple warheads. China is also building the DF-41 missile with a range of 12,000 kilometers (7,500 miles).[105] (The DF-41 will eventually replace the DF-5 ICBM.) If deployed, the DF-31 and the DF-41 will make China only the second country after Russia to deploy mobile long-range missiles.[106]

The new Type 094 nuclear submarine is expected to be completed by the year 2005; it will carry 16 Julang-2 missiles (a sea-based version of DF-31 missiles) with a striking range of 8,000 kilometers (5,000 miles). It has been reported that China is also attempting to develop a multiple, independently targeted reentry vehicle (MIRV).[107]

Some studies estimate that by 2010, China will increase the number of its ICBMs to 50–70, with MIRVed missiles deployed on mobile launchers and in hardened silos. It may deploy up to six second-generation SSBNs equipped with MIRVed missiles that can reach targets 8,000 kilometers (5,000 miles) away. This sea power will enable China to cover most of Asia, especially locations close to the Chinese mainland. In addition, China will possess a large number of tactical nuclear weapons with ranges of up to 900 kilometers (600 miles).[108]

According to a *Xinhua* report, China has built two special wind tunnels in Sichuan Province for testing its space shuttle, carrier rockets, and strategic missiles.[109] In 1999, China will attempt to launch its first manned spaceship.[110]

In early 1998, the PLA conducted a round of exercises whose purpose, according to Chinese officials, was to prepare the country to win a regional war through the use of high-tech weapons. PLA military commands also opened training classes across the country in which senior officers learned about advanced military technology. The last massive military exercises were held in the 1980s to coordinate all services and to enhance the command skills of PLA officers.[111] Yet, as one weapons specialist commented, the PLA still needs to improve its readiness for C^3I (command, control, communications, and intelligence).

It is worth noting that military experts, such as those proficient in guided-missile technology, have begun to serve at the decision-making level of combat units in the Second Artillery. Chinese political leaders believe that military technological expertise can help reduce errors in policy making and that it will play a significant role in promoting the modernization of Chinese nuclear forces.[112] That indicates that although the PLA has lost some political power in the most recent government reform, it is gaining more influence on China's defense decision making, including such critical decisions as China's response to India's nuclear development.[113]

TABLE 3
Chinese Strategic Nuclear Forces, 2005–2010

Type	Range/Payload (Km/Kg)	Total Forces 1998	Total Forces 2005–2010
Land-Based Ballistic Missiles			
DF-3/3A (CSS-2)	DF-3: 2,650/2,150 DF-3A: 2,800/2,150 Warhead: 3.3 MT	38	38+
DF-4 (CSS-3)	4,750/2,200 Warhead: 3.3 MT	10+	~10
DF-5/5A (CSS-4)	DF-5: 12,000/3,200 DF-5A: 13,000/3,200 Warhead: 4–5 MT	~20	~28
DF-21/21A (CSS-5)	DF-21: 1,700/600 DF-21A: 1,800/600 Warhead: 200–300 KT	30	30+
DF-31	8,000/700 Warhead: 100–200 KT	Under development	N/A
DF-41	12,000/800	Under development	22+
Strategic Submarines and Submarine-Launched Ballistic Missiles			
Julang-1 (CSS-N-3)	1,700/600 Warhead: 200–300 KT	12	~12
Julang-2	8,000/700 Warhead: 100–200 KT	Under development	<96
SSBN	N/A	1	<6

Note: Nuclear warhead yields are expressed in kilotons (KT) and megatons (MT), indicating an explosive force equivalent to that amount of TNT.

Sources: Estimates are based on data in Jones and McDonough, *Tracking Nuclear Proliferation, 1998,* p. 63; William M. Arkin, Robert S. Norris, and Joshua Handler, *Taking Stock: Worldwide Nuclear Deployments, 1998* (Washington, D.C.: National Resources Defense Council); Patrick J. Garrity, "Nuclear Weapons and Asia-Pacific Security: Issues, Trends, and Uncertainties," *National Security Studies Quarterly,* vol. IV, issue 1, Winter 1998, p. 46; Bill Gertz, "China Adds 6 ICBMs to Arsenal," *Washington Times,* July 21, 1998 (Internet edition); "New Declassified 1998 Report on the Ballistic Missile Threat," *Proliferation Brief,* (Washington, D.C.: Carnegie Endowment for International Peace), vol. 1, no. 13, September 28, 1998.

The current Chinese plan for nuclear modernization was not explicitly designed to counter a nuclear threat from India. Nonetheless, the possibility that its southern neighbor is developing nuclear weapons and delivery systems has given new urgency to Chinese debates about upgrading its nuclear forces. Since the Ninth National People's Congress in March 1998, China has restructured its nuclear-weapon policy-making community, enacted systematic new rules on nuclear exports, and taken other initiatives to confront the new threat to its security. A closer look at China's internal policy structure will help explicate these developments.

Internal Policy Structure

The National People's Congress, the highest organ of state power, decides on questions of war and peace and other defense-related issues. The president of the state proclaims a state of war. The State Council directs and administers national defense, and the Central Military Commission (a civilian agency) commands the nation's armed forces, including its nuclear forces.[114] In other words, the civilian government exercises tight control over the PLA.

At the operating level, the PLA is organized into four parts: the General Staff Department, the General Political Department, the General Logistics Department, and the General Armament Department, the last of which was established in April 1998 to integrate the country's historically separate ground, naval, and air forces' logistics and equipment purchases, to simplify joint operational procedures, and to reduce unnecessary expenditure.[115] (The nuclear forces, the so-called Second Artillery, are often not listed as a separate service, but they must have had similar problems, because they too are now under the joint system.)

The establishment of the General Armament Department is both a military reform and part of the defense modernization. As one of its officers said in June 1998, the PLA needs to follow—and to match—military modernization trends in other countries and to prepare for the future possibility of high-tech wars. The establishment of the department, according to this officer, facilitates united leadership by the Central Military Commission over weaponry and equipment building.[116]

General Cao Gangchuan is director of the General Armament Department; Lieutenant General Li Jinai is its political commissar.

Interestingly, both officials were former heads of COSTIND, which itself has undergone a major restructuring. Whereas in the past COSTIND was responsible both to the State Council and to the Central Military Commission, it now reports only to the State Council. Liu Jibin, the current minister of COSTIND, is a civilian (unlike General Cao Gangchuan, his predecessor). According to Liu, the reorganized COSTIND has three functions: to administer the national defense industry formerly under the administration of the old commission, to administer national defense construction formerly under the administration of the National Defense Department of the State Planning Commission, and to assume all the functions of five former big corporations—the China National Nuclear Corporation, Aviation Industries of China, China Aerospace Corporation, China North Industries Group, and China State Shipbuilding Corporation.[117] COSTIND is also empowered to make laws and regulations for defense science and technology development, to supervise the management of science and technology for national defense, and to draw up development plans for weapons production and research.[118] According to this author's interviews in Beijing in October 1998, the PLA now orders armaments from COSTIND.

As one General Armament Department officer pointed out, the establishment of that department and the reorganization of COSTIND are expected to change fundamentally the country's defense industrial structure and its weaponry and equipment management.[119] The change denotes the strengthening of civilian leadership over the PLA. It probably will take some time for the two new organizations to develop a smooth working relationship. The international significance of the domestic restructuring is that China may now be more able to implement nuclear security regimes effectively.

Corresponding to the structural adjustments, China has also taken executive and legislative measures to tighten its nuclear export controls. In May 1997, the State Council issued a Circular on Strict Implementation of China's Nuclear Export Policy. China claims that it follows three principles with respect to nuclear exports: that it exports nuclear materials for peaceful purposes only; that it accepts the supervision and safeguards of the IAEA; and that it forbids the transfer of nuclear materials to any third country without its consent. In addition, the circular emphasized that, "the nuclear materials, nuclear equipment and related technology, as well as non-nuclear materials for reactors and nuclear-related dual-use equipment, materials and relevant technologies on China's export list must not be supplied to or used in nuclear facilities not subject to IAEA inspections. No agency or company is allowed to conduct cooperation or exchange of personnel and technological data with nuclear facilities not under IAEA inspections."[120]

In September 1997, the State Council issued a Regulation on Nuclear Export Control, calling it "another important step" in enhancing and improving the management of China's nuclear exports. The regulation stipulates that nuclear exports will be the responsibility of departments appointed by the State Council; no other departments and individuals are allowed to engage in related activities. The Chinese government retains the right to terminate the export of approved nuclear materials if the recipient violates the regulation or if there is any danger of nuclear proliferation.[121]

In establishing a law on nuclear non-proliferation, China has referred to international norms and the U.S. model. In April 1998, a Chinese delegation visited the United States to study the U.S. nuclear-export-control law and categories of banned or restricted items. An official in Beijing said, "An export law which is a national law passed by the Standing Committee of the National People's Congress has much greater power than a regulation concerning enforcement of non-proliferation." He added that violators could face lawsuit and criminal punishment. The official said, however, that China would not allow American personnel to inspect enterprises suspected of exporting banned nuclear items, which he claimed "would infringe our sovereign rights."[122]

The record of Chinese nuclear proliferation has been the focus of sharp criticism by the United States and is a sore spot in U.S.-Chinese relations. At the same time, legal reforms in China to tighten nuclear-export controls have not received necessary attention in the United States. Among the most comprehensive of these reforms are the Regulations for Controlling the Export of Dual-Use Nuclear Goods and Relevant Technologies, issued by the State Council of the PRC in June 1998. The regulations stipulate that:

- The state exercise strict control over the export of dual-use nuclear goods and related technologies, and that it strictly abide by the international obligations it undertakes not to proliferate nuclear weapons;

- The state implement the system of licensing the export of dual-use nuclear goods and related technologies;
- The licensing system shall adhere to the following guidelines: (1) the recipient guarantees not to use dual-use nuclear goods and related technologies from China to conduct nuclear explosions, (2) the recipient guarantees not to apply dual-use nuclear goods and related technologies from China in nuclear facilities not safeguarded and supervised by the IAEA, and (3) the recipient guarantees not to transfer Chinese dual-use nuclear goods and related technologies to a third party without the Chinese government's consent;
- Parties engaged in exporting dual-use nuclear goods and related technologies shall register at the Ministry of Foreign Trade and Economic Cooperation. Without registration, no unit or individual may export dual-use nuclear goods and related technologies;
- The Ministry of Foreign Trade and Economic Cooperation shall submit applications to the State Council for approval of exports of dual-use nuclear goods and related technologies that have a major impact on national security, public interests, and foreign policy;
- The Ministry of Foreign Trade and Economic Cooperation, after consulting the Ministry of Foreign Affairs and the State Atomic Energy Authority, may suspend or revoke the export license of a party that violates its guarantees or presents the danger of nuclear proliferation;
- Any individual who violates the regulations and whose conduct constitutes a crime will face criminal prosecution.[123]

Despite existing controversies about China's missile and nuclear proliferation, the evidence also suggests that China is taking systematic measures to fulfill its international obligations. The international community has criticized China's strategic ambiguity and ineffective export-control mechanisms. The ongoing military reforms and the publication of the white paper discussed above are certainly steps in the right direction.

China will most likely maintain its current policy of limited warfare and limited nuclear deterrence over the next five years. Fundamentally, Beijing still considers economic development its top priority. To achieve a higher level of economic modernization, China needs both time and a stable environment. The Chinese leadership decided long ago how to apportion its financial resources between economic development and improvements in its nuclear force. At the same time, China seems to believe that it is not in its interest to assist any new nuclear-weapon power along its borders, including Pakistan. The administrative and legal establishment of new nuclear-export controls may help reduce the organizational disorder that existed in the past.

As one Indian scholar noted, "despite the entire exercise of nuclear testing being justified on the basis of the China factor, China's response has been very encouraging, gradual, and very balanced. [It is] the country most affected by India's tests and could have reacted in still worse manner." Commenting on China's nuclear transfer to Pakistan, some scholars believe that China has played "a subtle balancing game and done nothing that would radically change the balance of power on the [South Asian] subcontinent."[124]

NUCLEAR BUILDUP

It is hard to imagine that China would do nothing if India deployed a significant number of nuclear weapons or targeted nuclear weapons at China. Under the second scenario, one should expect China at a minimum to move its own warheads toward India. Pressure from the PLA would probably precipitate an additional buildup to maintain China's current nuclear advantage.

The Impact of Possible Indian Nuclear Deployments

A 1997 report by the U.S. Department of Defense stated that India might have a stockpile of fissile material sufficient for producing several nuclear weapons that could be assembled in a short time. Other analyses indicate that as of 1995, India had enough weapons-grade plutonium to produce at least sixty-five early-generation nuclear weapons.[125] Since 1983, India has launched an Integrated Guided Missiles Development Program aimed at the indigenous design and production of two major missile systems; these are now expected to be completed and deployed within five years (see Table 4).

Since the nuclear tests in May 1998, Indian leaders have made no secret of their intention to rely on nuclear weapons as a means of

TABLE 4
Indian Missile Programs

Name and Type	Features
Agni intermediate range ballistic missile	First test flight in 1989; striking range 1,500–2,500 km; demonstrated reentry capability; Agni II estimated range, 3,500 km.
Prithvi surface-to-surface tactical missile	First test flight in 1988; striking range 150–250 km; controlled and guided from launch to target.

Source: R. K. Jasbir Singh, ed., *Indian Defense Year Book 1997–98* (Dehra Dun: Indian Defense Year Book, 1997), pp. 495–503.

national security. This, of course, represents a fundamental shift in India's strategy. Jaswant Singh, senior adviser on defense and foreign affairs to Indian Prime Minister Vajpayee, explicitly expressed India's view that, "nuclear weapons remain a key indicator of state power" and that nuclear deterrence will work for India as it has for the West.[126] Many Indians still believe that China is a constant source of danger and that India must develop the capability of deterring a Chinese missile attack on India.[127]

If India does deploy nuclear weapons, it is conceivable that it will follow other nuclear-weapon powers in building a nuclear triad consisting of land-based missiles, bombers, and submarines. It is well known that nuclear technology and facilities can be used for both civilian and military purposes. According to one account, if the Indians add their commercial-reactor plutonium to their fissile material, they can build at least 390 and perhaps as many as 470 nuclear weapons, making India a larger nuclear force than Britain and on the same level as France and China.[128]

Among the three components of a potential Indian nuclear triad, the air force will perhaps become the earliest delivery option for nuclear weapons. It is interesting to note that in 1974, when India conducted its first nuclear test, its air force acquired the Anglo-French Jaguar, a deep-penetration strike aircraft capable of conducting nuclear missions. Later, India purchased Mig-27 and Mirage-2000 aircraft, both of which could be used to carry nuclear bombs. None of these aircraft could fly deep into China.

After India conducted the 1998 nuclear tests, its government approved the purchase of ten Su-30 aircraft, in addition to the forty it already had. Some of these aircraft have superior avionics and weapons systems. The Indian air force will upgrade these aircraft, but it has made no mention of using them for nuclear missions.[129] Acquisition of the Su-27, with a flight range that could cover most of China, would give the Indian air force a strategic strike capability.[130]

Traditionally, India has considered itself a maritime power. With Russian assistance, India plans to develop another arm of its nuclear triad, using Soviet-built C-Class nuclear submarines as a prototype for upgraded Indian versions that will carry at least six ballistic missiles. The first of five new Indian submarines are expected to be commissioned before 2004.[131] According to a recent news story, India will build a 2,500-ton attack submarine based on the design of French Rubis-class vessels, also by 2004.[132]

The Indian navy is building and buying large warships capable of both nuclear and conventional warfare. India is also preparing to construct a 30,000–50,000 ton aircraft carrier and will purchase another from Russia.[133] According to one report, negotiations for the Indian purchase of the *Admiral Gorshkov*, a Russian aircraft carrier, were well underway in late 1998.[134] Thus, tactical nuclear strike capabilities, which would certainly create a formidable nuclear threat to China, clearly seem to be part of Indian planning.

In the immediate aftermath of the nuclear tests, Indian leaders were presented with a series of vital questions concerning their future nuclear doctrine.[135] A few months later, New Delhi still has made no mention of the control, size, and composition of its nuclear arsenal.[136] All these developments will be carefully monitored in Beijing with the belief that the target of any new deployments will be China.

A Moderate Buildup

Since the end of the cold war, China has maintained relatively stable relationships with both Russia and the United States. Taking advantage of a generally peaceful international environment, China has set the recovery of Taiwan as a top priority. The PLA has focused more on limited, local warfare than on broad, international conflicts—a strategic shift that began in 1985. It has trained its forces and has purchased advanced armaments from Russia to support a possible operation against Taiwan. PLA missile exercises in the Taiwan Straits in 1995–1996 triggered the deployment of two U.S. aircraft carriers to the area, and the presence of U.S. forces in East Asia remains a key consideration in Chinese planning.

The 1998 Indian nuclear tests, and the potential threat they present to China's southwest borders, add a new concern for PLA military strategists. According to officials interviewed in Beijing in the fall of 1998, the Central Military Commission wants to maintain its focus on Taiwan and the South China Sea, but many military researchers expect the PLA to shift more forces to deal with India and Japan. Such a new military posture toward India was under active consideration at several military institutes, including the NDU, CIISS, and the China Defense Science and Technology Information Center.

For a long time, India has accused China of deploying nuclear weapons in Tibet, which has one of the world's richest deposits of uranium. The Dalai Lama has even asserted that China has operated at least one-third of its nuclear weapons in Tibet. (The Ninth Academy, China's primary weapons-development facility, was once located in Tibet's northeastern Amdo.[137])

In May 1998, George Fernandes, Indian defense minister, said that, "China has its nuclear weapons stockpiled in Tibet along India's borders."[138] A Chinese defense adviser and several nuclear scientists in Beijing said in October 1998, however, that China never deployed nuclear weapons in Tibet because of what they called the geographical difficulties of doing so. Nor does China need to do so, since its long-range missiles can reach India from far outside of Tibet. (They also asserted that the Ninth Academy was not in Tibet, but in China's Qinghai Province.) After India's nuclear tests, however, it seems more likely that China will deploy nuclear weapons in Tibet to strengthen its defense against India. At 4,000 meters above sea level and facing down on India, the Tibetan plateau is ideal for weapons deployment (the steep Indian side of the Himalayan border, by contrast, is not favorable to missile launches). Most Chinese defense analysts agreed that India has the upper hand in conventional military forces along the border. In response to India's nuclear moves, China would definitely take countermeasures, according to these experts.

China also can enhance its nuclear launch sites in Gansu, Qinghai, and Yunan provinces (see Table 1), where intermediate and long-range missiles are able to reach most parts of India. In the next five years, these missile launch sites will constitute a credible retaliatory strike force against India because India's nuclear capabilities could not effectively eliminate the Chinese nuclear deployments in those mountain areas.

Under this scenario, China is also likely to produce and deploy tactical nuclear weapons. In 1984, the U.S. Defense Intelligence Agency said that China did not seem to possess a tactical nuclear-weapons stockpile or to have developed a "coherent doctrine for tactical nuclear fire support of ground forces." A weapons development expert in Beijing also denied the existence of tactical nuclear weapons in China in late 1998, citing the high cost of producing small nuclear weapons.[139] But Chinese defense experts acknowledged their research on tactical nuclear weapons, and predicted that China would deploy such weapons if India does.

Shortly before India's nuclear tests in May, Defense Minister Fernandes said, "There can be no letup in our defense priorities as far as China is concerned. . . . We need to strengthen our positions along the borders with China."[140] Chinese military and diplomatic experts worried that India might provoke new incidents—and, in the worst case, a new war—along the Sino-Indian border for domestic political reasons. They also believe that India's conventional forces have outstripped the PLA and even have superiority in logistic support in the border region. PLA forces in the Chengdu Military Region have reportedly taken measures to defend the Tibetan border from Indian attack.[141]

According to interview respondents, China will answer any Indian nuclear deployment by targeting additional nuclear weapons (including tactical weapons) toward India and by trying to develop a missile-defense system. (In this regard, China is particularly interested in Russia's S-300 air-defense systems.) But China will not shift its nuclear doctrine or non-proliferation policy, nor will it massively build up its nuclear forces.

The debate on the appropriate Chinese response to the Indian nuclear threat illustrates the differences between China's civilian and military policy makers. Experts in civilian institutes, including CASS, CICIR, IAPCM, and CIIS argue that:

- India's nuclear tests did not pose a serious threat to China's national security;
- India's total power is much smaller than China's;
- China does not need to upgrade its nuclear forces to deal with India in the next five years because it will take a long time for India to develop its nuclear devices into usable weapons;
- China will cooperate with other nuclear powers and will use multilateral mechanisms to constrain India's nuclear threat.

Representatives of military institutes such as CIISS and CDSTIC argue that:

- China's deployment along the borders with India has traditionally been insufficient;
- India's nuclear tests have created a significant threat to China;
- China should respond by a moderate buildup of its nuclear forces;
- China should deploy nuclear weapons against India if India deploys them against China.

Of course, the civil-military division is not clear-cut. Some experts at the National Defense University suggested that the PLA does not have a common view on how best to counter the Indian threat. There is consensus within the Chinese military, however, that internal and external threats to China's west, including Tibet and Xinjiang, are real. All the major Chinese military institutes, and even some civilian institutes, are studying the effects of developments in India, Pakistan, and Afghanistan on China's security. In 1998, Jiang Zemin, Chinese president, met with leaders of the Tibet military region—an indication of the strategic importance of the Chinese west.[142]

REVERSAL OF THE COMMITMENT

China's commitment to the international non-proliferation regime is strong, but not irreversible. Under the third scenario, the deployment of missile-defense systems in Japan or Taiwan, coupled with the Indian nuclear and missile deployments noted above and a U.S. retreat from its policy of phased nuclear reductions (as embodied in the START treaty and the CTBT) could compel China to reverse course. China could refuse to ratify the Comprehensive Test Ban Treaty, for example, particularly if the U.S. Senate rejects the agreement and India also refuses to sign. It could decide not to join the Missile Technology Control Regime or to drop its diplomatic support for the Non-Proliferation Treaty. (Even if China does not withdraw from the NPT, it could join other nations in the developing world in criticizing the treaty's failure to accelerate nuclear disarmament.) In such a situation, the PLA is likely to play an even greater role in China's security decision making.

During an interview in October 1998, one PLA officer said that if the international non-proliferation system changes to accept India, China will adjust its nuclear policy. A senior Chinese diplomat also said that India's entrance into the nuclear club would mean the collapse of the non-proliferation regime.

The attitudes of Chinese experts toward nuclear non-proliferation regimes are mixed; some are more suspicious than others and even oppose the CTBT. In 1996, Chu Shulong and Yang Bojiang, senior fellows at CICIR, wrote that the United States provides Japan not only with a "nuclear defense capability" but also with a "nuclear attack capability." And while Japan's narrow territory may not be suitable for nuclear tests, that country's super computers are capable of simulating nuclear-test explosions.[143]

According to a Carnegie Endowment study, Japan's plutonium stocks will accumulate to between 11 and 25 tons by the year 2000, and to 50–80 tons by the year 2010. In addition to its current supplies of reactor-grade plutonium, Japan potentially could produce weapons-grade plutonium from its reactors now used for generating electricity, or by separating the super-grade plutonium produced in fast breeder reactors.

Japan's space program could also be converted into a missile development program. Japan has successfully tested the J-1 and M-5 solid-fueled rocket systems, which have payloads and ranges similar to U.S. ICBMs. A converted M-5 would be similar to the MX Peacekeeper, the largest operational U.S. ICBM. A converted J-1 missile would surpass the performance of a Minuteman 3. (The Minuteman and the Peacekeeper have striking ranges of 8,000 miles and 7,400 miles, respectively.)[144]

In addition to Japan's nuclear potential, China is increasingly concerned about a joint U.S.-Japan theater missile defense. The congressional Commission to Assess the Ballistic Missile Threat to the United States (the Rumsfeld Commission) concluded in July 1998 that China poses a threat both in nuclear weapons and in proliferation.[145] Many in the United States have advocated the deployment of theater missile defenses in East Asia against North Korea, Russia, and China. Since the United States initiated the discussion of missile defense in 1993, the Chinese have paid close attention to its development. Concerned that missile defenses would neutralize China's strategic nuclear deterrent, PLA analysts suggest that China and other countries will take countermeasures, resulting in a new Asian arms race.[146] In particular, as some American analysts point out, "transfer of upper tier systems [of theater missile defenses] with potential for strategic defensive applications to Japan would strongly compel Beijing's attention, because the Chinese would be likely to see such systems as contributing to a Japanese strategic shield behind which Tokyo might develop its own nuclear capabilities." Similarly, U.S. provision of missile defenses to Taiwan would undercut China's ability to intimidate Taiwan and would encourage Taiwan's independence movement.[147]

In the wake of a missile test by North Korea on August 31, 1998, China warned against "any country precipitating the arms race under the pretext of countering" North Korea's missiles. Even in this context, China opposed the decision by the United States and Japan to pursue joint missile-defense programs.[148]

In January 1999, Secretary of Defense William Cohen alarmed Beijing with his announcement that the United States would substantially increase funding both for a National Missile Defense system and for theater missile defenses. Cohen also suggested that the United States would try to convince Russia to amend the Anti-Ballistic Missile Treaty, and that if these efforts failed, the United States might pull out of the treaty.

In early February, military authorities in Taiwan claimed that the PLA had deployed more than 100 M-9 and M-11 missiles across the straits from Taiwan. Tang Fei, Taiwan's minister of defense, warned that the threat of China's guided missiles "has an impact not only on the military front but also on the political, economic, and psychological fronts."[149]

It is not certain whether Taiwan or Japan will actually deploy missile defenses, given the technical and budgetary problems they would have to overcome to do so. Secretary of State Madeleine Albright suggested during her visit to Beijing in early March 1999 that if the missile threat from China and North Korea were reduced, the need for missile defenses in East Asia would diminish.[150] In defense of their missile deployments, Chinese military officials claim that, "the objective of the buildup is to reinforce the effectiveness of the mainland's deterrence tactics." They argue, moreover, that the deployment of M-9 and M-11 missiles in coastal regions is a response to the new U.S. emphasis on missile defenses, which Beijing sees as a threat to the mainland.[151] Although the M-class missiles are nuclear-capable, China has deployed these short-range missiles only with conventional payloads. China is not known to have ever planned to use nuclear weapons against Taiwan, an area China considers part of its national territory.

The Chinese message has been clear: the deployment of missile defenses in East Asia could trigger the proliferation of conventional and strategic military weaponry and would constitute a new threat to the region. The inclusion of Taiwan in U.S. missile defense networks, a PLA newspaper warned, "will meet strong objection from the Chinese people."[152] The Ministry of Foreign Affairs also warned of "grave consequences if the missile-defense system is implemented in Asia, and specifically if Taiwan is allowed to participate in it."[153]

China is also afraid of the other major powers resuming nuclear tests, both real and computer-simulated. Sun Xuegui, a Chinese defense expert, argued in a January 1997 publication that both before and after the signing of the CTBT, the Chinese government exhibited a willingness to compromise on almost all major issues. But passage of the treaty signified only the end of actual nuclear explosions, not the end of nuclear-weapon experiments, much less the disappearance of the threat of nuclear war. New high-speed computers offer the United States a means to simulate explosions. The use of these new methods of nuclear testing by Western powers could possibly lead to a nuclear race at a higher level, Sun concluded.[154]

Fu Chengli, another defense analyst writing in January 1997, claimed that the United States had indicated its ability to conduct simulated nuclear tests and had even hinted at a possible withdrawal from the CTBT treaty after ten years. According to Fu, the United

States, which once actively advocated a nuclear test ban, now appears prepared to conduct formal nuclear tests if such testing is deemed necessary to ensure its nuclear predominance. Fu's article offers a stark view of Chinese security concerns and helps explain why some Chinese analysts would urge reversing the implementation of the CTBT if they perceive China's security is jeopardized by its weakened nuclear power.[155]

5
Implications of China's Nuclear Policy for Other Countries

The primary focus of this study has been China's recent reactions and possible future responses to the 1998 South Asian nuclear tests. This chapter briefly considers the implications of China's nuclear policy for four other countries, each of which has substantial interaction with China on national-security issues.

JAPAN

Although Japan is commonly regarded as an economic, not a military, powerhouse, the country's conventional forces actually rank among the best in the world. The Japanese navy projects formidable power in the South China Sea, passage for more than 80 percent of Japan's oil supplies. Close ties to Indonesia assure access to other key sea lanes in Southeast Asia.

The 1998 Indian nuclear tests are a potential threat to Japan's strategic interests. Some analysts suggest that if India were to develop a fleet of nuclear-armed submarines, for example, it could project greater force throughout the region, possibly preventing the passage of Japanese oil ships at the Andaman Sea or the Strait of Malacca (which would force costly rerouting elsewhere).[156] It was not surprising, therefore, that Ryutaro Hashimoto, Japanese prime minister, condemned the Indian blasts as "extremely regrettable" or that Japan shortly thereafter imposed economic sanctions on India.[157]

Japan also joined the United States in seeking China's intercession to prevent the subsequent Pakistani nuclear tests.[158]

The Sino-Japanese relationship, however, is much more complex than any other bilateral relationships of the two countries. Although it is unthinkable that China would use nuclear weapons against Japan, Japan feels extremely uneasy with the status quo; it advocates a faster pace of disarmament leading to a nuclear-weapon-free Asia and, in the meantime, a missile-defense system for itself.

The deepening economic recession in 1998 seemed to weaken Japan's international political standing as well. The country was rebuffed in its request to participate in a June 1998 meeting in Geneva, when the foreign ministers of the five permanent members of the UN Security Council attempted to coordinate a response to the South Asian nuclear tests. Many Japanese felt that their country had been slighted and blamed China in particular for excluding Japan from this meeting.[159]

At present, the Japanese-Chinese bilateral relationship remains stable and the two countries have not entered any kind of arms race. Japan possesses the upper hand in high-tech conventional forces, while China's advantage lies in its nuclear weapons. (This balance of power may shift if Japan deploys a missile-defense system. And Japan has the technical potential to become a nuclear-weapon power, if it so chooses.) In principle, both countries agree on the desirability of eliminating nuclear weapons worldwide.

RUSSIA

Sino-Russian relations have improved throughout the 1990s. The two countries signed a series of agreements to settle their border disputes; bilateral trade increased and broadened; and their top leaders held summits almost every year. The armed forces of both countries have left only limited defensive troops along the borders, have stopped targeting nuclear weapons at each other, and have mutually agreed on no first use of nuclear forces.

As China modernizes its military, it will continue to look to Russia for assistance. Chinese purchases of Russian military technology include Mi-8 transport helicopters, Mi-17 transport and assault helicopters, S-300 PMU surface-to-air missiles, Kilo-class submarines, Sovremmeny-class guided-missile destroyers, Su-27 fighters, Il-76M transport aircraft, and Phalcon/Beriev AWACS (airborne warning and control system) aircraft.

Russia and China coordinated their responses after India and Pakistan conducted nuclear tests, when both countries urged New Delhi and Islamabad to enter into the CTBT and the NPT unconditionally. Russia and China also refused to acknowledge the South Asian countries as nuclear-weapon states.[160] There are, however, potential frictions between the two over future developments in South Asia. In June 1998, Russia signed a $2.6 billion agreement to build two Indian nuclear-power reactors, sending what many observers called the wrong signal at the wrong time.[161] Russia is also helping India develop nuclear-powered submarines. Although Russia may not be motivated by an anti-China strategy, its support for India's nuclear power program will most likely become an issue between Beijing and Moscow.

NORTH KOREA

Two days after India's tests, North Korea caught the world's attention by threatening to revive its own nuclear program. The North Korean ambassador to China told reporters in Beijing that some officials in his country had called for the reopening of nuclear facilities that had been closed in 1994 according to an agreement between North Korea and the United States.[162] On August 31, 1998, North Korea launched an IRBM with what it called a satellite over Japan's territory, prompting Keizo Obuchi, Japanese prime minister, to say that Japan might launch a reconnaissance satellite of its own over North Korea.[163]

Despite China's reaction to South Asia's nuclear tests and its confirmed commitment to non-proliferation on the Korean Peninsula, it is unclear how much influence China can actually exert on its North Korean ally. It is suspected that Chinese leaders did not receive any prior notice of the August launch and were not even sure whether North Korea launched a missile or a satellite.[164]

In the future, China will continue its policy of trying to persuade North Korea to give up its nuclear-weapon program, while also cautioning other countries against using North Korean developments as a reason for building missile-defense systems in East Asia.

UNITED STATES

One of the few positive consequences of the 1998 South Asian nuclear tests is the opportunity it presents for a new strategic partnership between the United States and China. China has long exerted diplomatic pressure on New Dehli to work with the United States to terminate India's nuclear-weapon development. In early June 1998, the foreign ministers of China and the United States met in Geneva with their counterparts from Russia, France, and Britain (the other three declared nuclear-weapon states) to discuss the nuclear crisis in South Asia. Chinese Foreign Minister Tang Jiaxuan chaired this meeting. Its final communiqué urged India and Pakistan to sign the CTBT unconditionally and to refrain from deploying nuclear-armed missiles.[165]

U.S. President Bill Clinton visited China in late June–early July 1998, at which time a Sino-U.S. Presidential Joint Statement on South Asia was released. Among its key assertions are the following:

> "Our shared interests in a peaceful and stable South Asia and in a strong global non-proliferation regime have been put at risk by these tests, which we have joined in condemning. . . . China and the United States remain firmly committed to strong and effective international cooperation on nuclear non-proliferation, with the NPT as its cornerstone. . . . We reaffirm that our respective policies are to prevent the export of equipment, materials, or technology that could in any way assist programs in India or Pakistan for nuclear weapons, and that to this end, we will strengthen our national export control systems."[166]

During the Jiang–Clinton summit in Beijing, the two leaders also signed a pledge not to target strategic nuclear weapons at each other. In late July, Foreign Minister Tang gave Madeleine Albright, U.S. Secretary of State, new assurances that his government would follow through on this promise. Both sides also renewed their commitment to press India and Pakistan to stop developing nuclear armaments.[167]

The recent increase in Islamic activities against the Chinese government in Western China highlights another area where U.S. and

Chinese interests in non-proliferation coincide. With tensions grow-
ing on its own borders, China does not want to see a nuclear-armed
Pakistan. At Clinton's request, President Jiang urged the Pakistani
government not to go ahead with its tests a few days before Pakistan
exploded nuclear devices in May.[168] China continues to pressure that
country not to transfer nuclear weapons or technology to other
Central Asian and Middle Eastern nations.

Throughout the 1990s, China has also distanced itself from North
Korea, a historic ally, and has quietly pressured Pyongyang to give
up its nuclear-weapon program and to engage in peace talks with
South Korea and the United States.[169] Shortly after the South Asian
nuclear tests, the North Korean regime threatened to reopen nuclear
power facilities it closed under international pressure in 1994 (and
which were later reported to be a cover for a nuclear-weapon program).[170] In late 1998, the United States, China, and the two Koreas
began a third round of negotiations on procedures that could lead
to a peace treaty to replace the armistice that has existed since the
end of the Korean War in 1953.[171]

Relations between the U.S. military and the PLA have also
improved in recent years, as exemplified by high-level military visits,
professional and educational exchanges, and increased consultation
on maritime military security. U.S. warships and aircraft continue
to berth in Hong Kong since its return to China from Britain in July
1997.[172] And, according to an interview in Beijing in October 1998,
the United States and China are actively considering a joint sea
exercise in the near future.

Despite these favorable developments, a number of sore points
exist in the developing Sino-U.S. strategic partnership. As recently
as October 1998, representatives of all of the major civilian and
military Chinese institutes voiced suspicion that the United States
had helped India conduct its nuclear tests in May to constrain the
growth of China's power. These experts also did not believe that
the Central Intelligence Agency could have failed to detect prepara-
tions for the tests. Chinese analysts also pointed to several U.S.
government documents that continue to describe China as a potential
threat, not an ally.

China and the United States have profound conflicts of interest
on the Taiwan issue. While the mainland Chinese are supportive of
the NPT and CTBT, most of them argued that the United States

must reduce its arms sales to Taiwan, which they view as another kind of proliferation, before China will sign the MTCR. The Chinese also are aware of statements by U.S. officials like John Holum, acting undersecretary of state for arms control and international security affairs, who testified before the U.S. Senate that, "the United States has a very strict policy, secured in a bilateral technology safeguards agreement between the U.S. and China, designed to prevent the transfer of sensitive missile technology to China that could assist its space launch vehicle program."[173]

Finally, U.S. and Chinese domestic politics will continue to play a role in Sino-U.S. relations. Many policy makers in Washington argue that China will use the developments in South Asia as an excuse to build up its own nuclear forces. From the perspective of non-proliferation, however, the current state of Sino-U.S. relations presents a rare opportunity for an improved partnership between these two major powers. Future debates on promoting both U.S. and Asian security should consider the following factors:

- The current Chinese debate on the South Asian nuclear tests is not about a new nuclear doctrine or proliferation policy, but about the appropriate Chinese response to India's nuclear-weapon development. At a time when China's civilian and military policy makers seem divided over what to do, the United States should try to help China regain a sense of confidence in its own security environment so that it will not reverse its commitments to nuclear regimes or increase its nuclear forces.
- China is facing a dilemma in its relations with Islamic countries. Despite traditionally close relationships with countries such as Pakistan and Iran, China is trying its best to prevent the proliferation of nuclear weapons to the Islamic world (and to North Korea).
- The United States can use cooperation on non-proliferation as a testing ground for an expanded Sino-U.S. strategic partnership. A genuine partnership cannot develop if both countries are still at odds over the nuclear issue, but a comprehensive strategic partnership could lead to important new areas of cooperation on non-proliferation and other pressing issues.

6
What Next?

At present, China will likely maintain its current state of nuclear forces and commitment to non-proliferation. Nevertheless, developments in East and South Asia may force a change in China's current posture. For most countries, ratification of the Non-Proliferation Treaty means adherence to the norm that no more states should develop or acquire nuclear weapons beyond the five that conducted nuclear tests before 1967. At the same time, the NPT does not legitimize the privilege of permanent possession of nuclear weapons by any state. While the ultimate goal of arms control remains the elimination of the nuclear threat altogether, the intermediate goal remains non-proliferation. The 1998 tests by India and Pakistan present a clear challenge to the non-proliferation regime. There are sound reasons for all nations to uphold, expand, and strengthen this regime. Among the most important steps that should be taken to accomplish this are the following:

- The United States should work to strengthen the Non-Proliferation Treaty and to bring into force the Comprehensive Test Ban Treaty. To demonstrate its leadership, the U.S. Senate should ratify the CTBT as soon as possible, a move that would greatly enhance the effectiveness of the nuclear non-proliferation regime.
- The United States and Russia should proceed with the Strategic Arms Reduction Treaty process, and China, France, and Britain should likewise begin to negotiate reductions of their own nuclear forces. Each phase, of course, requires prudent execution at no cost to national or international security (by giving the wrong signal to aspiring nuclear proliferants, for example).

- The Non-Proliferation Treaty should be kept intact. No revisions should be made to enlarge the existing nuclear-weapon club. A relaxed rule would be misleading for other potential nuclear-weapon states and would cause a new round of crisis for the non-proliferation regime.
- The nuclear non-proliferation regime needs to be reexamined from the supply side. Export controls on dual-use nuclear technology must be universal among all nuclear-weapon states and not discriminate against non-nuclear-weapon countries. Meanwhile, the security concerns of non-nuclear-weapon states need to be addressed.

At present, it seems that India and Pakistan are intent on deploying nuclear weapons whether or not they are formally recognized as nuclear-weapon states under the NPT. Many have criticized as unrealistic the intention of the United States and other countries to roll back the proliferation of nuclear weapons in South Asia. The choice for the international community is either to redouble its efforts to contain the spread of nuclear weapons—or to abandon the nuclear non-proliferation regime as unworkable.

China has committed itself to the Comprehensive Test Ban and is not likely to resume nuclear tests for a long time. Nevertheless, China might continue the proliferation of nuclear technology and devices that are restricted by the NPT either intentionally or because of loopholes in its export-control system. China also is almost certain to delay joining the Missile Technology Control Regime.

To influence Chinese behavior in the future, U.S. policy makers should first put the Chinese situation in context: China's proliferation has been motivated primarily by its broader thinking on, among other issues, Taiwan, Japan, and the Persian Gulf. Taiwan is both a security concern and a matter of great political importance to China—a point often lost on those in Washington who miss the clear causal relationship between China's proliferation and U.S. arms sale to Taiwan.

The United States and China obviously have areas where their interests are in conflict—and areas where their interests overlap. The United States should continue to encourage China to abide by the regimes on test ban, nuclear export control, and pledges not to target nuclear weapons at each other, with appropriate inspection mechanisms wherever applicable.

Finally, the United States should develop a routine dialogue with China at the cabinet level—and higher—to improve mutual understanding and to reduce existing differences. Working together, the two countries can do much to repair the non-proliferation regime and to improve peace and stability in South Asia.

Notes

1. Robert Norris, Andrew Burrows, and Richard Fieldhouse, eds., *Nuclear Weapons Databook, Vol. V: British, French, and Chinese Nuclear Weapons* (Boulder, Colo.: Westview Press, 1994), pp. 359, 372.

2. Robert Walpole, national intelligence officer for strategic and nuclear programs, Central Intelligence Agency, presentation at the Carnegie Endowment for International Peace, September 17, 1998, summarized in "New Declassified 1998 Report on the Ballistic Missile Threat," *Proliferation Brief* (Washington, D.C.: Carnegie Endowment Non-Proliferation Program), vol. 1, no. 13, September 28, 1998.

3. International Institute for Strategic Studies, *The Military Balance 1997–98* (London: International Institute for Strategic Studies, 1998), p. 178.

4. Norris, Burrows, and Fieldhouse, 1994, pp. 365–368.

5. Rodney W. Jones and Mark G. McDonough, *Tracking Nuclear Proliferation: A Guide in Maps and Charts, 1998* (Washington, D.C.: Carnegie Endowment for International Peace, 1998), p. 63.

6. *Defense Working Paper* (Washington, D.C.: Progressive Policy Institute), no. 4, April 1998. See also Hans Binnendijk and Ronald Montaperto, eds., *Strategic Trends in China* (Washington, D.C.: National Defense University Press, 1998), p. 22.

7. Avery Goldstein, "Great Expectations: Interpreting China's Arrival," *International Security*, vol. 22, no. 3, Winter 1997/98, p. 49.

8. Liu Hongji and Luo Haiyi, eds., *Guofang Lilun* (National Defense Theory) (Beijing: National Defense University Press, 1996).

9. Alastair Iain Johnston, "China's New 'Old Thinking': The Concept of Limited Deterrence," *International Security*, vol. 20, no. 3, Winter 1995/96, pp. 5–42; Hongxun Hua, "China's Strategic Missile Programs: Limited Aims, Not 'Limited Deterrence,'" *Nonproliferation Review*, Winter 1998, pp. 60–68.

10. Liu and Luo, 1996, pp. 163–8.

11. The concept referred to missiles capable of reaching a range of at least 300 kilometers (190 miles) with a payload of at least 500 kilograms.

12. Based on data compiled by the East Asia Nonproliferation Project, Center for Nonproliferation Studies, Monterey Institute of International Studies (Monterey, Calif., November 1997).

13. See database published on the Internet website of the Center for Nonproliferation Studies, Monterey Institute of International Studies (www.cns.miis.edu).

14. "The Issue of Nuclear Weapons," *China's National Defense* (Information Office of the State Council, People's Republic of China), as published on the Internet website of the Embassy of the People's Republic of China in the United States (www.china-embassy.org/Cgi-Bin/Press.pl?wparms), July 1998.

15. Information Office of the State Council, People's Republic of China, Internet website of the Embassy of the People's Republic of China in the United States. (A negative security guarantee is a pledge made by nuclear-weapon powers not to use or threaten to use nuclear weapons against non-nuclear-weapon countries; a positive security guarantee is a promise by nuclear countries to provide active assistance to non-nuclear-weapon states if they are subject to aggression in which nuclear weapons are used.)

16. Ibid.

17. Melvyn C. Goldstein, "Tibet, China, and the United States: Reflections on the Tibet Question," occasional paper (Washington, D.C.: Atlantic Council of the United States), April 1995.

18. Peng Jichao, "He Yinyingxia de Shijie Fengyun" (The Century under the Nuclear Shadow), *Xiandaihua* (Modernization), no. 4, 1996, p. 8.

19. Rodney W. Jones, "India," in Jozef Goldbalt, ed., *Non-Proliferation: The Why and the Wherefore* (London: Taylor and Francis, 1985), pp. 101–123.

20. Ye Zhengjia, "China's Experience in Conflict Avoidance and Confidence Building with India," as published in the Southern Asia Internet Forum, Henry L. Stimson Center (www.stimson.org), November 12, 1997 .

21. Sony Devabhaktuni, Matthew C.J. Rudolph, and Amit Sevak, "Key Developments in the Sino-Indian CBM Process," occasional

paper (Washington, D.C.: Henry L. Stimson Center, 1998), pp. 201–204.

22. Ibid., pp. 203–204.

23. Raju G. C. Thomas, *South Asian Security in the 1990s* (London: International Institute for Strategic Studies, *Adelphi Paper* 278, July 1993), pp. 64, 70.

24. J. Mohan Malik, "China-India Relations in the Post-Soviet Era: The Continuing Rivalry," *China Quarterly*, June 1995, p. 322.

25. Cited in Neil Joeck, *Maintaining Nuclear Stability in South Asia* (London: International Institute for Strategic Studies, *Adelphi Paper* 312, 1997), p. 37.

26. Krishnaswami Sundarji, "Proliferation of WMD and the Security Dimensions in South Asia: An Indian View," in Stuart E. Johnson and William H. Lewis, eds., *Weapons of Mass Destruction: New Perspectives on Counterproliferation* (Washington, D.C.: National Defense University Press, 1995), p. 58.

27. *India Today*, May 18, 1998, p. 22.

28. *South China Morning Post*, Internet edition, May 4, 1998.

29. *India Today*, May 18, 1998, pp. 18, 22.

30. *New York Times*, May 13, 1998, p. A12.

31. *The Times of India*, May 15, 1998.

32. *The Hindu*, Internet edition, May 15, 1998; *India Today*, May 18, 1998, p. 20.

33. *India Today*, May 18, 1998, p. 23.

34. *India Today*, May 18, 1998, p. 24.

35. Raj Chengappa and Manoj Joshi, "Hawkish India," *India Today*, June 1, 1998, p. 30.

36. *Foreign Broadcast Information Service–China-98-138 Daily Report*, May 19, 1998 (hereafter cited as *FBIS-CHI*).

37. *FBIS-CHI 98-140 Daily Report*, May 21, 1998. Most Western scholars attribute ten nuclear-power plants, nine heavy-water plants, four reprocessing facilities, and three uranium-enrichment plants to India.

38. M. G. Chitkara, *Toxic Tibet Under Nuclear China* (New Delhi: APH Publishing Corporation, 1996), p. 112.

39. *FBIS-CHI-98-152 Daily Report*, June 2, 1998.

40. Chengappa and Joshi, p. 30.

41. *Foreign Broadcast Information Service–Near East and South Asia-98-219 Daily Report*, August 10, 1998 (hereafter cited as *FBIS-NES*).

42. *Washington Post*, December 16, 1998, p. A37.

43. Zou Yunhua, "Chinese Perspectives on South Asian Nuclear Tests" (Stanford: Center for International Security and Cooperation, January 1999), p. 15.

44. Kenneth J. Cooper, "Indian-Pakistani Cold War Shifts to Nuclear Matchup," *Washington Post*, April 5, 1996, p. A21.

45. John Ward Anderson, "Confusion Dominates Arms Race," *Washington Post*, June 1, 1998, p. A1.

46. Bill Gertz, "Pakistan Braced for Strike on Eve of Nuclear Tests," *Washington Times*, Internet edition, June 1, 1998. Other evidence suggests that Washington and Beijing do not necessarily worry about an immediate nuclear exchange in South Asia. *Xinhua* cited Pentagon spokesman Kenneth Bacon as saying that, "We do not see any evidence that they are moving toward a nuclear exchange." He added that, "Both sides are working on long-range missiles, and that is worrisome." See *FBIS-CHI-98-149*, June 1, 1998.

47. *FBIS-CHI-98-230 Daily Report*, August 19, 1998.

48. Barbara Crossette, "India Vetos Pact to Forbid Testing of Nuclear Arms," *New York Times*, Internet edition, August 21, 1996.

49. India claimed that it conducted three nuclear tests on May 11, 1998, including a thermonuclear device (that is, a hydrogen bomb) that had a much larger yield than the 1974 explosion. The other two tests were of a low-yield device like the one tested in 1974 and a fission device. But U.S. officials suggested that the total force of the three Indian tests ranged from 10 to 20 kilotons of TNT, roughly the same amount as the 1974 explosion. On May 13, defying worldwide condemnation of these tests, India conducted two more underground nuclear tests and once again caught the world by surprise. The two tests, according to Indian government, had an explosive force of less than 1,000 tons of TNT, significantly lower than the first round of tests. See Kenneth J. Cooper, "India Sets Off Nuclear Devices," *Washington Post*, May 12, 1998, p. A1; R. Jeffrey Smith, "India Sets Off Nuclear Devices," *Washington Post*, May 12, 1998, p. A1; and Kenneth J. Cooper, "India Conducts 2nd Round of Nuclear Tests," *Washington Post*, May 14, 1998, p. A1.

50. Personal interview, Beijing, October 1998.

51. Personal interviews, Washington and Beijing, July 1996 and October 1998.

52. David Shambaugh, "China's Commander-in-Chief: Jiang Zemin and the PLA," in Dennison Lane, Mark Weisenbloom, and

Dimon Liu, eds., *Chinese Military Modernization* (Washington, D.C.: AEI Press, 1996), p. 235.

53. *FBIS-CHI-97-159 Daily Report,* June 10, 1997.

54. Personal interviews, Washington and Beijing, July 1996 and October 1998.

55. Michael Swaine, *The Role of the Chinese Military in National Security Policymaking* (Santa Monica: RAND Corporation, 1996), pp. 69–70.

56. Ibid., p. 69.

57. *FBIS-CHI-98-132 Daily Report,* May 13, 1998.

58. *FBIS-CHI-98-132 Daily Report,* May 13, 1998.

59. *FBIS-CHI-98-133 Daily Report,* May 15, 1998.

60. *FBIS-CHI-98-141 Daily Report,* May 23, 1998.

61. *South China Morning Post,* June 2, 1998; *Hong Kong Standard,* June 3, 1998.

62. *FBIS-CHI-98-154 Daily Report,* June 4, 1998.

63. *FBIS-CHI-98-187 Daily Report,* July 7, 1998.

64. *FBIS-CHI-98-190 Daily Report,* July 10, 1998.

65. *FBIS-CHI-98-191 Daily Report,* July 13, 1998.

66. *FBIS-CHI-98-142 Daily Report,* May 26, 1998.

67. *FBIS-CHI-98-209 Daily Report,* July 29, 1998.

68. *FBIS-CHI-98-155 Daily Report,* June 5, 1998.

69. *FBIS-CHI-98-156 Daily Report,* June 8, 1998.

70. *FBIS-CHI-98-206 Daily Report,* July 28, 1998.

71. *FBIS-CHI-98-191 Daily Report,* July 13, 1998.

72. *FBIS-CHI-98-207 Daily Report,* July 28, 1998.

73. *FBIS-CHI-98-220 Daily Report,* August 11, 1998.

74. *FBIS-CHI-98-219 Daily Report,* August 10, 1998.

75. Dong Guozheng, "Hegemonist Ambition Is Completely Exposed," *Liberation Army Daily,* May 19, 1998, p. 5; *FBIS-CHI-98-140 Daily Report,* May 21, 1998.

76. Liu Yang and Guo Feng, "What Is the Intention of Wantonly Engaging in Military Ventures—India's Military Development Should Be Watched Out For," *Liberation Army Daily,* May 19, 1998, p. 5; *FBIS-CHI-98-141 Daily Report,* May 23, 1998.

77. *FBIS-CHI-98-204 Daily Report,* July 27, 1998.

78. "Interview with Yang Haisheng," *Liberation Army Daily,* May 25, 1998, p. 5; *FBIS-CHI-98-152 Daily Report,* June 2, 1998.

79. *FBIS-CHI-98-161 Daily Report,* June 11, 1998.

80. *The Hindu*, Internet edition, June 18, 1998.

81. *Washington Times*, Internet edition, May 18, 1998.

82. John Ward Anderson and Kamran Khan, "Pakistan Sets Off Nuclear Blasts," *Washington Post*, May 29, 1998, p. A1.

83. Ibid.

84. Steve Coll, "'Dr. Strangelove' Enlists the Subcontinent," *Washington Post*, May 29, 1998, p. A1.

85. Abdul Qadeer Khan, the mastermind of Pakistan's nuclear program, told reporters that all the devices tested were of the fission type, as opposed to more powerful fusion, or thermonuclear, weapons. The first five tests included "a big bomb which had a yield of about 30–35 kilotons, which was twice as big as the one dropped on Hiroshima." The other four tests were of low yield and for tactical weapons. Some U.S. military and intelligence officials said that they detected only a single weak seismic signal from the Pakistani test site; U.S. analysts estimated that the first test on May 28 was of two bombs with a total explosive force of six kilotons of TNT. The second test on May 30 was even smaller. U.S. analysts also had doubts about India's claim to have tested a thermonuclear device. See Molly Moore, "'Father of the Islamic Bomb' Defends Role," *Washington Post*, June 1, 1998, p. A14.

86. Stephen Kinzer, "Chinese Assurances Could Avert Pakistani Nuclear Testing," *New York Times*, Internet edition, May 19, 1998.

87. *FBIS-CHI-98-138 Daily Report*, May 19, 1998.

88. *FBIS-CHI-98-139 Daily Report*, May 21, 1998.

89. *FBIS-CHI-98-140 Daily Report*, May 21, 1998.

90. Elisabeth Rosenthal, "China, Key Ally of Pakistan, Voices 'Regret,'" *New York Times*, Internet edition, May 29, 1998.

91. *FBIS-CHI-98-148 Daily Report*, May 29, 1998.

92. Elisabeth Rosenthal, May 29, 1998.

93. John Pomfret, "China Asked Pakistan Not to Conduct Tests," *Washington Post*, May 29, 1998, p. A36.

94. *China Daily*, Internet edition, June 3, 1998.

95. *FBIS-CHI-98-237 Daily Report*, August 26, 1998.

96. Song Yichang, "Lengzhan Yifeng Heshi Liao" (When Will the Wind of Cold War End), *Jianchuan Zhishi* (Naval and Merchant Ships), No. 226, July 1998, p. 15.

97. Tian Dongfeng, conference presentation, summarized in *Bulletin of the Center for American Studies*, Fudan University, no. 2, 1998.

98. Jin Yingzhong, conference presentation, summarized in *Bulletin of the Center for American Studies,* Fudan University, no. 2, 1998.

99. Information Office of the State Council, People's Republic of China, as published on the Internet website of the Embassy of the People's Republic of China in the United States (www.china-embassy.org/Cgi-Bin/Press.pl?wparms), July 1998.

100. Ibid.

101. *FBIS-CHI-98-243 Daily Report,* September 1, 1998.

102. Lisbeth Gronlund, David Wright, and Yong Liu, "China and a Fissile Material Production Cut-Off," *Survival,* vol. 37, no. 4, Winter 1995–96, pp. 150–151.

103. Bill Gertz, "China Adds 6 ICBMs to Arsenal," *Washington Times,* Internet edition, July 21, 1998.

104. Bill Gertz, "China Conducted Missile Test During Clinton Visit," *Washington Times,* Internet edition, July 22, 1998.

105. Jones and McDonough, 1998, pp. 55, 63.

106. Bill Gertz, "China Adds 6 ICBMs to Arsenal," *Washington Times,* Internet edition, July 21, 1998.

107. Jones and McDonough, 1998, pp. 55–64.

108. Patrick J. Garrity, "Nuclear Weapons and Asia-Pacific Security: Issues, Trends, and Uncertainties," *National Security Studies Quarterly,* vol. IV, issue 1, Winter 1998, p. 46.

109. *FBIS-CHI-98-110 Daily Report,* April 21, 1998.

110. Ibid.

111. *FBIS-CHI-98-102 Daily Report,* April 15, 1998.

112. *FBIS-CHI-98-176 Daily Report,* June 26, 1998.

113. PLA officers and analysts openly discuss issues such as the revolution in military affairs, information warfare, the security environment, and military theory in *Liberation Army Daily, China National Defense Daily,* and other professional journals.

114. *China's National Defense* (Information Office of the State Council, People's Republic of China, on website www.china-embassy.org/Cgi-Bin/Press.pl?wparms). It should be pointed out that the Standing Committee of the Political Bureau of the Chinese Communist Party still has the final say on all major security policies.

115. *FBIS-CHI-98-243 Daily Report,* September 1, 1998.

116. *FBIS-CHI-98-163 Daily Report,* June 15, 1998.

117. *FBIS-CHI-98-114 Daily Report,* April 28, 1998.

118. *FBIS-CHI-98-090 Daily Report,* April 2, 1998; *FBIS-CHI-98-119 Daily Report,* May 1, 1998.

119. *FBIS-CHI-98-163 Daily Report*, June 15, 1998.

120. Jiang Wandi, "Tighter Controls on Nuclear Exports," *Beijing Review*, no. 48, December 1–7, 1997, pp. 21–22.

121. *FBIS-CHI-97-258 Daily Report*, September 16, 1997.

122. V. P. K. Chan, "Beijing Bases New Nuclear Anti-Proliferation Law on U.S. Model," *South China Morning Post*, Internet edition, April 23, 1998.

123. *Xinhua*, Beijing, June 17, 1998.

124. Swaran Singh, May 15, 1998; Gaurav Kampani, June 5, 1998, as published on the Internet website of the South Asia Internet Forum, Henry L. Stimson Center (www.stimson.org).

125. Office of Secretary of Defense, *Proliferation: Threat and Response*, November 1997; Jones and McDonough, p. 111.

126. Jaswant Singh, "Against Nuclear Apartheid," *Foreign Affairs*, vol. 77, no. 5, September/October 1998, pp. 43–44.

127. *FBIS-NES-98-226 Daily Report*, August 17, 1998.

128. Waheguru Pal Singh Sidhu, presentation at the Carnegie Endowment for International Peace Non-Proliferation Forum, "India's Nuclear Force and Use Doctrine," July 16, 1998 (on website www.ceip.org/programs/npp/sasial.html).

129. *FBIS-NES-98-240 Daily Report*, August 31, 1998.

130. Sidhu, 1998.

131. Zhang Minhui, "He Shiyan Hou de Yin Ba Haijun" (Indian and Pakistani Navies after Nuclear Tests), *Naval and Merchant Ships*, July 1998, p. 18.

132. Kevin Sullivan, "Indian Nuclear Sub Plan Reported," *Washington Post*, June 27, 1998, p. A20.

133. Zhang, 1998, p. 18.

134. *FBIS-NES-98-225 Daily Report*, August 14, 1998.

135. Kenneth J. Cooper, "Nuclear Dilemmas," *Washington Post*, May 25, 1998, pp. A1, A22.

136. Pamela Constable, "India Plays Nuclear Waiting Game," *Washington Post*, September 14, 1998, p. A15.

137. Chitkara, 1996, pp. 43, 47.

138. *South China Morning Post*, Internet edition, May 4, 1998.

139. China has clearly demonstrated its interest in tactical nuclear weapons and may already have deployed some kinds of atomic demolition munitions, nuclear artillery, Multiple-Rocket System shells, or tactical missiles. DF-15 and DF-11 short-range missiles are

all nuclear-capable and would be useful in a border war with India. See Norris, Burrows, and Fieldhouse, 1994, pp. 370–371.

140. *South China Morning Post*, Internet edition, May 7, 1998.

141. *FBIS-CHI-98-264 Daily Report*, September 22, 1998.

142. According to a news report, the Central Military Commission sent additional troops into Xinjiang to deal with possible ethnic riots in July and August 1998. *FBIS-CHI-98-287 Daily Report*, October 16, 1998.

143. "U.S. Nuclear Protection and Japanese Nuclear Intention," *People's Daily*, June 20, 1996.

144. Selig S. Harrison, "Overview," in Selig S. Harrison, ed., *Japan's Nuclear Future* (Washington, D.C.: Carnegie Endowment for International Peace, 1996), pp. 18–19, 21.

145. *Executive Summary of the Report of the Commission to Assess the Ballistic Missile Threat to the United States*, as published on the Internet website of the U.S. Congress, House of Representatives, Committee on Armed Services (www.house.gov/hasc/testimony/105th congress/BMThreat.htm), July 15, 1998.

146. Theresa Hitchens and Naoaki Usui, "China Sees Japan's TMD as Threat to Nuclear Might," *Defense News Weekly*, April 22–28, 1996, pp. 12, 26; Zhang Yeliang, "Meiguo Zhangqu Daodan Fangyu Jihua yu Lengzhan hou Guoji Anquan" (U.S. TMD and Post Cold War International Security), no. 5, 1997, p. 36.

147. Binnendijk and Montaperto, "Introduction;" Michael Nacht, "Nuclear Issues," in Binnendijk and Montaperto, 1998, pp. 21, 83.

148. China Daily, Internet edition, September 23, 1998.

149. John Pomfret, " China Aims More Missiles at Taiwan," *Washington Post*, February 11, 1999, Internet edition.

150. Jane Perlez, "China Syndrome: Disputes Persist, Civility Rules," *New York Times*, March 3, 1999, Internet edition.

151. Oliver Chou, "Missile Force 'Response to Threat,'" *South China Morning Post*, Internet edition, February 11, 1999.

152. *Jiefangjun Bao*, January 24, 1999, p. 4.

153. John Pomfret, February 11, 1999.

154. Sun Xuegui, "Thinking after the Passage of 'the Comprehensive Nuclear Test Ban Treaty' in the United Nations General Assembly," *CONMILIT*, January 1997, p. 25.

155. Fu Chengli, "Review of the 1996 World Military Situation," *CONMILIT*, January 1997, pp. 10–13.

156. Song, 1998, p. 13; Yoichi Funabashi, "Tokyo's Depression Diplomacy," *Foreign Affairs*, vol. 77, no. 6, November/December 1998, p. 29.

157. Kamran Khan and Kevin Sullivan, "Indian Blasts Bring World Condemnation," *Washington Post*, May 13, 1998, p. A1.

158. *FBIS-EAS-98-136 Daily Report*, May 19, 1998.

159. Funabashi, 1998, p. 31.

160. *China Press* (in Chinese), July 23, 1998, p. 2.

161. *Newsbrief*, Programme for Promoting Nuclear Non-Proliferation (Mountbatten Centre for International Studies, University of Southhampton, UK), no. 43, 1998, p. 5.

162. Kevin Sullivan, "N. Korea Threatens Revival of its Nuclear Program," *Washington Post*, May 15, 1998, p. A33.

163. Nicholas D. Kristof, "Japan May Launch a Satellite in Response to North Korea's," *New York Times*, Internet edition, September 11, 1998.

164. "Mainland Baffled by North Korea Missile," *Hong Kong Standard*, Internet edition, September 9, 1998.

165. *FBIS-CHI-98-152 Daily Report*, June 2, 1998; CNN, "Big 5 Nuclear Powers Convene to Discuss India, Pakistan," Internet edition, June 4, 1998.

166. *FBIS-CHI-98-178 Daily Report*, June 30, 1998.

167. "Beijing to Honor Joint Arms Pledge," *Hong Kong Standard*, Internet edition, July 28, 1998.

168. John Pomfret, "China Asked Pakistan Not to Conduct Tests," *Washington Post*, May 29, 1998, p. A36.

169. Ming Zhang, "The New Mission of the Chinese Communist Party: A Revisit to Communist International Relations," *Journal of Communist Studies and Transition Politics*, vol. 13, no. 4, December 1997, pp. 79–98.

170. Elizabeth Olsen, "U.S., China and the 2 Koreas Take a First Step Toward Peace," *New York Times*, Internet edition, October 25, 1998.

171. Elizabeth Olsen, October 25, 1998.

172. *FBIS-CHI-98-170 Daily Report*, June 22, 1998.

173. John D. Holum, "Remarks on Technology Transfers to China," U.S. Senate Committee on Commerce, Science, and Transportation, September 17, 1998.

Appendix A

China's Participation and Positions Regarding Nuclear Arms Control and Non-Proliferation Regimes

Regimes	Chinese Participation and Positions	Dates of Participation
Nuclear-Weapon-Free Zones (NWFZs)	Stated support	1964
Conference on Disarmament	Yes	1980–present
International Atomic Energy Agency (IAEA)	Yes	Applied September 1983; member January 1, 1984
Convention on Assistance in the Case of a Nuclear Accident or Radiological Emergency	Yes	Signed September 26, 1986; ratified September 10, 1987
Convention on the Early Notification of a Nuclear Accident	Yes	Signed September 26, 1986; ratified September 10, 1987
Convention on the Physical Protection of Nuclear Material	Yes	Acceded to January 10, 1989
Missile Technology Control Regime (MTCR)	Adherent	Written assurance (to the United States), February 1992; agreed to study MTCR membership actively, June 27, 1998
Non-Proliferation Treaty (NPT)	Yes	Acceded to March 9, 1992; supported decision to extend indefinitely the NPT in April 1995
London Convention (on nuclear dumping)	Yes	Adherence since February 21, 1994

Regimes	Chinese Participation and Positions	Dates of Participation
Detargeting agreements	Yes (with Russia and the United States)	With Russia, September 3, 1994; with the United States, June 27, 1998
Convention on Nuclear Safety	Yes	Signed September 20, 1994; ratified April 6, 1996; entered into force October 24, 1996
Comprehensive Test Ban Treaty (CTBT)	Signed; not yet ratified	Signed September 24, 1996
Zangger Committee	Yes	Joined October 16, 1997
No-First-Use (NFU) and Negative/Positive Security Assurances (N/PSA)	Stated support	NFU treaty presented January 1994; N/PSA presented July 1998
Fissile Material Cut-off Treaty (FMCT)	Stated support for the negotiation of a treaty	N/A
Joint Convention on the Safety of Spent Fuel Management and on the Safety of Radioactive Waste Management	No	N/A
Korean Peninsula Energy Development Organization (KEDO)	No (but has stated support for Korean denuclearization)	N/A
Nuclear Suppliers Group (NSG)	No	N/A
Peaceful Nuclear Explosions Treaty	No	N/A

Source: Based on databases compiled by the Center for Nonproliferation Studies, Monterey Institute for International Studies, January 1999.

Appendix B

Ambassador Sha Zukang on the Non-Proliferation Regime

Ambassador Sha Zukang, director-general of the Department of Arms Control and Disarmament at China's Ministry of Foreign Affairs, discussed China's non-proliferation policy and its views on the current state of the non-proliferation regime at the Seventh Carnegie International Non-Proliferation Conference on January 12, 1999, in Washington, D.C. An edited version of Ambassador Sha's address follows.

The good momentum of the international non-proliferation efforts maintained since the end of the cold war was severely interrupted by the Indian and Pakistani nuclear tests last May. How to repair and consolidate the damaged international non-proliferation regime is a pressing task facing us today. Whether we can cope with it effectively will have far-reaching impacts on the future development of the international situation. I would like to share with you some of my thoughts on this issue from the nuclear, biological, chemical, and missile perspectives.

The nuclear non-proliferation regime was the hardest hit by the Indian and Pakistani nuclear tests. It is of vital importance that further proliferation of nuclear weapons be prevented. To this end, first and foremost, we must exert all our efforts to stop and reverse the nuclear development programs of India and Pakistan. The Indian and Pakistani nuclear tests have presented the international community with both a challenge and an opportunity. In a sense, these events have become a litmus test of the effectiveness of the international non-proliferation regime. If the international community could take effective measures to stop or even to reverse the two countries' nuclear development programs, the authority and vitality of the international nuclear non-proliferation regime would be immeasurably enhanced.

To achieve this, two things are important. First, the international community should have sufficient patience and perseverance, and should not lose hope because of the lack of progress in the short run. Second, the international community, especially the major powers, must achieve consensus and take concerted action on this matter. A robust international non-proliferation regime is in the interests of all countries. If any country seeks to exploit the South Asian situation to obtain unilateral short-term political, economic, or strategic benefits at the expense of other countries and international solidarity, and in total disregard for the serious consequences the South Asian nuclear testing has had on the international non-proliferation regime, it can only further undermine the already badly damaged international non-proliferation regime, and, in the end, the long-term interests of that country will also be jeopardized. It is a direct violation of UN Security Council Resolution 1172 to negotiate, or even to discuss, with India on India's so-called minimum nuclear deterrence capability. It is also unhelpful to support publicly India's permanent membership in the UN Security Council soon after its nuclear tests. It is obvious that these actions will not help in repairing the damage caused by the South Asian nuclear tests to the international nuclear non-proliferation regime.

Secondly, the international nuclear non-proliferation regime should be replenished. At present, this includes three main aspects. First is the Comprehensive Nuclear Test-Ban Treaty (CTBT). All states concerned should sign and ratify the treaty as soon as possible, so that it can enter into force at an early date. China is accelerating its preparatory work and will submit the treaty to the People's Congress for ratification in the first part of this year, with the hope that the ratification procedures can be completed before September 1999. Second is the Fissile Material Cut-off Treaty (FMCT). Negotiation should start as soon as possible. All states should make the necessary efforts and demonstrate the necessary political will to conclude a good treaty at an early date, one which guarantees the adherence of all states capable of producing nuclear materials. The third aspect is to strengthen nuclear export control. China joined the Zangger Committee in October 1997, and has promulgated the regulations on Nuclear Export Control and on the Export Control of Nuclear Dual-Use Items and Related Technologies. For historical reasons, China has not joined the Nuclear Suppliers Group so far, but we support its non-proliferation objectives and have actually incorporated both of its control lists, in their entirety, into China's own national regulations. In this connection, we have noted with concern that after the Indian nuclear tests, some Nuclear Suppliers Group members have taken a more proactive stand on issues of nuclear cooperation with India. We hope that these countries could be more cautious in this area.

Thirdly, the nuclear disarmament process should be accelerated. The fundamental solution to nuclear proliferation lies with complete nuclear disarmament. We do not believe there exists a cause and effect relationship between the present lack of progress in nuclear disarmament and the Indian nuclear testing, as claimed by the Indian government. But, at the same time, we fully recognize that an accelerated pace of nuclear disarmament will certainly be conducive to consolidating the international non-proliferation regime. The United States and the Russian Federation are duty-bound to take the lead in nuclear disarmament. We hope that START II could be effective and implemented, and the negotiation on START III initiated, as soon as possible. On such basis, the two countries should further reduce their nuclear arsenals so as to prepare the ground for other nuclear-weapon states to join in the process.

Last but not least, the role of nuclear weapons should be further diminished. The nuclear-deterrence policy based on the first-use of nuclear weapons highlights the discriminatory nature of the existing nuclear non-proliferation regime, which does not help to strengthen the international nuclear non-proliferation regime or to dissipate the misconception of countries like India that the possession of nuclear weapons is a shortcut to the status of a world power. We are pleased to note that Germany and Canada have advocated that the North Atlantic Treaty Organization should abandon its policy of first use of nuclear weapons. We hope that positive results could come out of the on-going debates within NATO on this matter.

* * *

Compared with the nuclear non-proliferation regime, the international regime against the proliferation of chemical and biological weapons, which is based on the Chemical Weapons Convention

(CWC) and the Biological Weapons Convention (BWC), is more justified and less discriminatory, but it is by no means problem-free.

With respect to chemical weapons, the relationship between CWC and the Australia Group is a thorny issue. CWC, a treaty which was concluded after extended multilateral negotiations, and has as many as 121 state parties, contains clear provisions on the export of sensitive chemicals, accompanied with long schedules. We do not deny the right of any country to stipulate stricter export controls than those required by CWC, and to establish small groups for that purpose. However, the existence of the Australia Group has resulted in discrepancies in the legal provisions of different countries, which has created a de facto split legal system within the CWC state parties. This inevitably causes confusion and affects the normal international trade of chemicals. This problem is compounded by the seemingly irresistible inclination of certain countries to impose their own standards or even their own domestic legislation onto other countries, thus giving rise to unnecessary international disputes. All this has seriously undermined the authority of the CWC. As far as I can see, there are only two ways to rectify this situation: to dissolve the Australia Group or to amend the CWC to bring it in line with the requirements of the Australia Group. Anyway, there must be a single standard rather than two.

The faithful implementation of the existing international treaties is the prerequisite for the strengthening of the non-proliferation regime. CWC has been in force for almost two years, but a certain country has still not submitted its complete declarations, as required by the Convention, and has even passed its own national legislation which openly contravenes the provisions of the Convention. Such a practice of putting one's national legislation above the international law and refusing to fulfill one's obligations under an international treaty cannot but cause concern.

With respect to biological weapons, the negotiation on a protocol aimed at strengthening the BWC has entered its final stage. The establishment of any verification system should be guided by the principles of fairness, appropriateness, and effectiveness. Otherwise, verification weakens rather than strengthens the non-proliferation regime. In this connection, there are many lessons to be drawn from the weapons inspections in Iraq. We must have a realistic estimate of the role of verification. The purpose of verification is to deter potential violators from violating its obligations. At the same time, we should be realistic enough to see that no verification regime, however perfect or complete, can provide a 100-percent guarantee that no violations could happen. Therefore, verification measures should be appropriate and feasible. If they are too intrusive and affect the legitimate security or economic interest of the state parties, or are too costly and impossible to sustain in the long run, they will not be able to get widespread support, and in the end the universality of the treaties will be undermined, which in turn will be detrimental to the strengthening of the non-proliferation regime.

* * *

Devoid of any legal basis in international law, missile non-proliferation is the most underdeveloped part of the entire international non-proliferation regime. As the founders of the Missile Technology Control Regime (MTCR) admitted, MTCR is just a time-winning device. Its purpose is to delay missile proliferation rather than to provide a comprehensive solution to this problem. Even this limited role was somehow diminished by the regime's lack of objective criteria, and the double standard applied by certain MTCR members in implementing requirements of the regime. Recent developments have shown that the risk of missile proliferation is increasing. It is time for the international community to take a collective look at the missile proliferation issue, including MTCR, and to explore better ways to combat this danger.

One cannot discuss missile proliferation without mentioning theater missile defense (TMD). We are deeply concerned about certain countries' efforts to develop advanced TMD or even national missile defense (NMD), for the following reasons:

First, the development of advanced TMD or even NMD will have negative impacts on regional or even global strategic stability. Like nuclear weapons, missiles can proliferate both horizontally and vertically. If a country, in addition to its offensive power, seeks to develop advanced TMD or even NMD in an attempt to attain absolute security and unilateral strategic advantage for itself, other countries will be forced to develop more advanced offensive missiles. This will give rise to a new round of arms race which will be in no one's interest. To avoid such a situation, it is extremely important to maintain and strengthen the Anti-Ballistic Missile Treaty (ABM).

During the cold war, the ABM Treaty was one of the cornerstones of the strategic stability between the United States and the former Soviet Union, which made it possible for the two countries to make deep cuts in their respective nuclear arsenals. After the cold war, with the world moving rapidly toward multipolarity, the significance of the ABM Treaty has increased rather than decreased. Some scholars have put forward the idea of making the ABM Treaty a multilateral treaty. I think this is an idea worthy of our serious consideration.

Secondly, transferring TMD systems to other countries or regions or developing them jointly with other countries will inevitably result in the proliferation of missile technology. Missile and antimissile technologies are related. Many of the technologies used in antimissile systems are easily applicable in offensive missiles. This is one of the main reasons why China stands against the cooperation between the United States and Japan to develop TMD and opposes any transfer of TMD systems to Taiwan. We hope that the U.S. government would take a more cautious and responsible attitude on this matter. China's opposition to U.S. transfers of TMD to Taiwan is also based on another major concern, namely, its adverse impact on China's reunification. TMD in Taiwan will give the pro-independence forces in Taiwan a false sense of security, which may incite them to reckless moves. This can only lead to instability across the Taiwan Strait or even in the entire northeast Asian region.

In conclusion, I wish to emphasize that the proliferation problem cannot be solved without taking the large international environment into consideration. It is important that a fair and just new world order be established whereby all states treat each other with equality. The big and powerful should not bully the small and the weak. And all disputes should be solved peacefully, without resort to the use or threat of force. This is the most effective way to remove the fundamental motivations of countries to acquire weapons of mass destruction, and the best approach to non-proliferation.

Appendix C

Summary of China's Nuclear Weapons and Policies

The text below is excerpted from the chapter on China in Tracking Nuclear Proliferation, A Guide in Maps and Charts, 1998, *by Rodney W. Jones and Mark G. McDonough, with Toby F. Dalton and Gregory D. Koblentz, (Washington, D.C.: Carnegie Endowment for International Peace, 1998).*

China, a nuclear-weapon state since 1964, opened itself to wider exchange and trade in the late 1970s and began to export arms and military technology on a significant scale. It also became a supplier of sensitive nuclear technology. China's exports posed major problems for the non-proliferation regime both because of their indiscriminate nature and because of China's failure to apply the safeguards and controls exercised by states compliant with the Nuclear Non-Proliferation Treaty (NPT). As a result, the United States and other countries began sustained efforts to draw China into the international non-proliferation regime. Over the more than two decades since China's "opening," these efforts have achieved incremental but important progress.

Nonetheless, China continues to pose formidable challenges to the international non-proliferation regime. As a May 1996 Pentagon report points out, China has been a contributor to proliferation "primarily because of the role of Chinese companies in supplying a wide range of materials, equipment and technologies that could contribute to NBC [nuclear, biological, and chemical] weapons and missile programs in countries of proliferation concern." China disregarded international norms during the 1980s by selling nuclear materials to countries such as South Africa, India, Pakistan, and Argentina, without requiring that the items be placed under International

Atomic Energy Agency safeguards. Although China joined the NPT in 1992, and pledged to the United States in the same year and again in 1994 that it would abide by the Missile Technology Control Regime (MTCR), it was slow to adopt and publish nuclear export control laws.

China's nuclear exports to two particular countries, Pakistan and Iran, have been the leading causes of concern. Even though Pakistan is not a party to the NPT, has had a nuclear weapons program since 1972, and is believed to have had a small arsenal ready to assemble for a number of years, China has been its principal supplier of nuclear equipment and services since the late 1970s. Similarly, even though Iran is believed to have started a nuclear weapons program in the mid-1980s, China supplied it with key nuclear equipment. Although Iran is a member of the NPT, the United States has led an international effort to prevent the supply of nuclear technology to Iran and has placed pressure on China (and other suppliers) to cancel nuclear deals with Iran. With respect to China, by 1997 this U.S. pressure apparently had made a difference.

Missile Export Activities

In the missile export field, China reportedly has aided the missile programs of Libya, Saudi Arabia, Syria, Iraq, Iran, Pakistan, and possibly North Korea. In Pakistan's case, China evidently transferred key components in the early 1990s for short-range, nuclear-capable M-11 surface-to-surface missiles. In June 1991, the United States imposed MTCR Category II sanctions against entities in Pakistan and China for missile technology transfers. These sanctions were lifted in March 1992 after the United States received written confirmation from China that it would abide by the MTCR "guidelines and parameters." Washington took this oral confirmation to mean China would not export either the M-9 or the M-11 missile. Since the latest sanctions were lifted, however, several reports have emerged that China continues to aid Pakistan's and Iran's ballistic missile programs.

China's Fissile Material Stockpile

A frequently overlooked proliferation threat posed by China is the large stockpile of weapons-usable fissile material it has produced over the past thirty years. Although the situation in China currently seems more stable than in Russia, increased political and economic instability could raise the risk of diversion of fissile material from China's nuclear complex. The possibilities run the spectrum from a breakup of China into multiple states, the breakdown of central authority and the rise of regional warlords, or a steady deterioration of central authority that would increase the opportunity for theft and smuggling of nuclear material or weapons.

There are several unofficial estimates on how much weapons-usable fissile material China has produced, but Beijing has not disclosed the size of either its nuclear weapon or fissile material stockpiles. Experts believe that China has tested about forty-five nuclear explosive devices and built about 300 strategic warheads and 150 tactical warheads. Together with materials used in the fuel for civil and military reactors, a considerable portion of the fissile materials produced must have been consumed or must be otherwise unavailable for weapons. According to the most recent estimates, it is believed that by the end of 1994, China's residual fissile material stockpiles may consist of as much as 4 metric tons of plutonium and 23 metric tons of highly enriched uranium—enough fissile material for approximately 2,700 nuclear weapons.

Information on China's material protection, control, and accounting (MPC&A) system is scarce, but the United States has been concerned enough to initiate discussions on MPC&A, among other issues, between the U.S. and Chinese national nuclear laboratories. There have been contacts between the nuclear weapons laboratories in the United States and China since 1994, and five joint workshops were scheduled for 1996 with the Chinese Academy of Engineering Physics, China's main nuclear weapons research center. Although China's MPC&A system is modeled after the Soviet system, an expert at one of the U.S. national laboratories ranked China's MPC&A system as better than that of the Soviet Union before it collapsed. In 1996, China commissioned a computerized "national nuclear materials accounting system" at about twelve nuclear facilities to improve its ability to prevent the illegal loss, theft, or transfer of nuclear materials.

China's Nuclear Weapons

China's nuclear arsenal of approximately 450 weapons would make it the third largest nuclear military power today. China has only seven intercontinental ballistic missiles (ICBMs) capable of striking the continental United States (the DF-5s). It has a single nuclear submarine, the Xia, based on the Shandong Peninsula. China is currently modernizing its strategic missile force with three new solid-fuel ballistic missiles, including a submarine-launched missile. A new generation of nuclear-powered submarines (Type 094) reportedly are scheduled for construction after the year 2000 and would carry 16 JL-2 missiles. Some reports indicate that China's new DF-31 ICBMs, first tested in 1995, will be deployed with multiple warheads, but there has been no official confirmation that China has developed MIRV capability. China's attempts to acquire advanced SS-18 missile-guidance technology from Russia and Ukraine may have been linked to the pursuit of MIRV capability.

China has expressed concern that current U.S. missile defense programs could neutralize China's ICBMs, its principal strategic deterrent against the United States. The combination of a national missile defense covering the United States and the sale of advanced theater missile defense systems to America's Asian allies would greatly complicate China's nuclear planning. China has reportedly tested intermediate-range ballistic missiles with penetration aids to foil missile defenses, and similar measures are expected to be added to China's new generation of long-range ballistic missiles.

China's Non-Proliferation Commitments

With China an established nuclear-weapon state and permanent member of the UN Security Council, Beijing's nuclear policies, attitudes toward the non-proliferation effectiveness of export controls, and quality of participation in global non-proliferation regimes naturally carry weight in the decision making of other countries. Having been an outsider to most international arms control initiatives during the cold war, China never signed the 1963 Partial Test Ban Treaty, only became a member of the IAEA in 1984, acceded to the NPT as recently as 1992, declined until 1997 to join the international Zangger Committee, and still declines to join the Nuclear Suppliers Group. While it has agreed to observe the published MTCR guidelines of 1987, it still is not a full partner and may not be fully observant of the revised MTCR guidelines of 1993. It also may have a unilateral interpretation of certain MTCR guidelines. It is clear that China shuns "informal" multilateral control arrangements such as the NSG, MTCR, and, in the chemical weapons area, the Australia Group.

Nevertheless, China made notable strides to join formal arms control regimes in the 1990s—beginning with its accession to the NPT in 1992, its signature in 1993 and ratification in 1997 of the Chemical Weapons Convention (CWC), and its cessation of nuclear weapon explosive testing and signature of the Comprehensive Test Ban Treaty (CTBT) in September 1996. China has supported the multilateral negotiations on a fissile-material production cutoff convention. China also acceded to the Biological Weapons Convention (BWC) in 1984. Moreover, China has gradually clarified and upgraded the commitments it makes through export controls to nuclear and missile non-proliferation objectives. These nuclear export control clarifications and practical improvements are worthy of note, as are the areas of continued divergence.

Prospects

Compared with its past nuclear export practices, China appeared to have made decisive strides in recent years toward conforming its nuclear export policies, laws, and regulations to international standards. The primary remaining formal shortcomings are that: (1) China still has not agreed to accept full-scope safeguards as an export requirement and has not agreed to join the Nuclear Suppliers Group (which goes further than the Zangger Committee by upholding that requirement); (2) China has not publicly adopted a "catchall" obligation to deny nuclear or nuclear-related exports or assistance to a country that might satisfy formal IAEA and NPT criteria yet have a dubious non-proliferation record for other reasons; and (3) China has not yet demonstrated its commitment to vigilantly follow up and monitor the end-use assurances on its nuclear and nuclear-related exports within recipient states and facilities.

Moreover, formal adherence to legal standards is one thing, while effective enforcement of the underlying purposes is another. Past experience suggests that it will take some time to determine whether China's practices in nuclear exports and nuclear cooperation will meet international standards for nuclear-related and dual-use equipment, materials, and technology that could be used for nuclear weapon purposes. In addition, it is one thing for the government of China to promulgate new export control regulations and another to ensure that they are effectively enforced by obtaining the compliance of all nuclear-related domestic manufacturing and trading firms—many of which are connected with the military yet operate as profit centers or revenue-raising mechanisms—as well as the compliance of the more typical, public-sector scientific and technical organizations and laboratories.

The missile and chemical and biological areas will also require diligent attention. Up to 1994, China made progress on MTCR requirements. But it is still not clear that its professed restraint applies, as the MTCR requires, to missile components and technology—nor, indeed, that the restraint applies to more than complete "ground-to-ground" missiles. Compliance in this area, which is not defined by a treaty, is harder to nail down with standards that China can accept politically—and also entails more scope for ambiguities. The chemical area is defined by treaty, provides for declarations, and lists restricted items, but it covers a very large industrial domain. Considerable effort will be required to work out reliable non-proliferation standards in these areas. But progress with China in the nuclear areas should add confidence to such efforts in other areas.

About the Author

Ming Zhang is director of research at IHS International in Virginia and a consultant to the Carnegie Endowment for International Peace. He has been a visiting fellow at the Institute for National Strategic Studies of the National Defense University and a research analyst with the Library of Congress. Dr. Zhang studied history and international relations at Nanjing University, China, and at the Johns Hopkins Center in Nanjing. He earned his Ph.D. in political science from Purdue University in 1994.

Ming Zhang has contributed numerous articles to academic journals and edited anthologies. He is the author of *Major Powers at a Crossroads: Economic Interdependence and an Asia Pacific Security Community* (Lynne Rienner, 1995) and the coauthor of *A Triad of Another Kind: the United States, China, and Japan* (St. Martin's Press, 1999).

About the Non-Proliferation Project

The Non-Proliferation Project at the Carnegie Endowment for International Peace serves as an independent source of information and analysis on international security affairs and conducts a wide array of professional and public-education activities promoting international efforts to curb the spread of weapons of mass destruction.

In Washington, the Project's ongoing program of research and analysis includes two surveys: *Tracking Nuclear Proliferation*, a book-length periodic review of the global spread of nuclear arms, and *Nuclear Successor States of the Soviet Union: Status Report on Nuclear Weapons, Fissile Material, and Export Controls*, a report on nuclear controls and disarmament in the former Soviet Union (prepared with the Monterey Institute of International Studies).

The Project also sponsors Non-Proliferation Roundtables, a meeting series on current non-proliferation topics, convenes off-the-record discussions with top policy officials and experts, and distributes Proliferation Policy Briefs. It maintains an extensive site on the World Wide Web devoted to proliferation issues: www.ceip.org/npp.

In Moscow, the Project is conducting a series of activities promoting debate on non-proliferation policies and internal nuclear control measures in the former Soviet Union. Managed by Alexander Pikayev, scholar-in-residence at the Carnegie Moscow Center, these efforts include regular seminars with key Russian experts and officials, major conferences, and the publication of two Russian-language periodicals on non-proliferation.

The Non-Proliferation Project is directed by Joseph Cirincione, senior associate at the Carnegie Endowment. It is funded by generous contributions from the Carnegie Corporation of New York, the W. Alton Jones Foundation, the Ford Foundation, the John Merck Fund, the Prospect Hill Foundation, the Ploughshares Fund, and the Kendall Foundation.

The Carnegie Endowment for International Peace

The Carnegie Endowment was established in 1910 in Washington, D.C., with a gift from Andrew Carnegie. As a tax-exempt 501(c)(3) nonprofit organization, the Endowment conducts programs of research, discussion, publication, and education in international affairs and U.S. foreign policy. The Endowment publishes the quarterly magazine, *Foreign Policy*.

Carnegie's senior associates—whose backgrounds include government, journalism, law, academia, and public affairs—bring to their work substantial first-hand experience in foreign policy. Through writing, public and media appearances, study groups, and conferences, Carnegie associates seek to invigorate and extend both expert and public discussion on a wide range of international issues, including worldwide migration, nuclear non-proliferation, regional conflicts, multilateralism, democracy building, and the use of force. The Endowment also engages in and encourages projects designed to foster innovative contributions in international affairs.

In 1993, the Carnegie Endowment committed its resources to the establishment of a public policy research center in Moscow designed to promote intellectual collaboration among scholars and specialists in the United States, Russia, and other post-Soviet states. Together with the Endowment's associates in Washington, the center's staff of Russian and American specialists conduct programs on a broad range of major policy issues ranging from economic reform to civil-military relations. The Carnegie Moscow Center holds seminars, workshops, and study groups at which international participants from academia, government, journalism, the private sector, and non-governmental institutions gather to exchange views. It also provides a forum for prominent international figures to present their views to informed Moscow audiences. Associates of the center also host seminars in Kiev, Ukraine, on an equally broad set of topics.

The Endowment normally does not take institutional positions on public policy issues. It supports its activities principally from its own resources, supplemented by nongovernmental, philanthropic grants.

Carnegie Endowment
for International Peace
1779 Massachusetts Ave., N.W.
Washington, D.C. 20036
Tel: 202-483-7600
Fax: 202-483-1840
E-mail: carnegie@ceip.org
Web: www.ceip.org

Carnegie Moscow Center
Ul. Tverskaya 16/2
7th Floor
Moscow 103009
Tel: 7-095-935-8904
Fax: 7-095-935-8906
E-mail: info@carnegie.ru
Web: www.carnegie.ru

0 ____ 500
Miles

RUSSIA

KAZAKHSTAN

Lop Nur Nuclear Weapons Test Site. *Also possible site of nuclear weapons stockpile.*

MONGOLIA

Jiuq
Loca
proce
proce
hexa
Proc
weap
to ur
Com
work

KYRGYZSTAN

TAJIKISTAN

Malan ■

XINJIANG

Lop Nur

GANSU

Subei ■

Jiuquan ▲

Northwest Nuclear Weapons Research and Design Academy (Qinghai Academy).

Da Qaidam ▲
▲ *Xiao Qaidam*
▲ *Delingha*

Haiyan ■ ▲
D

QINGHAI

PAKISTAN

Lanzhou Gaseous Diffusion Plant. *China's main facility for producing weapons grade uranium; possible pilot-scale commercial reprocessing plant under construction.*

Guangyuan. *Site of China's largest plutonium production reactor and plutonium separation (reprocessing) plant, believed to be the main hub of nuclear weapons production in China.*

TIBET

NEPAL

Large-scale uranium enrichment plant; under construction.

BHUTAN

INDIA

BANGLA-DESH

YUN

Heping. *Site of China's second gaseous diffusion uranium enrichment plant; can produce between 750 and 2,950 kg of weapons-grade uranium per year.*

■ *Nuclear weapons research or production*

▲ *Missile deployment or air base*

(See associated charts for site-specific details)

MYANMAR (BURMA)

Carnegie Endowment for International Peace, *Tracking Nuclear Proliferation*, 1998

SOURCES: Robert S. Norris et al., Nuclear Weapons Databook, Natural Resources Defense Council, March 1994; and "Datafile: China,"

China Nuclear Energy Industry Corporation. *Commercial arm of the government-owned China National Nuclear Corp. Sold ring magnets manufactured at the Yibin plant to Pakistan in 1994-95.*

...lan Atomic Energy Complex. *...tion of plutonium production, ...ssing and fabrication facilities, ...ssing plant for uranium ...luoride, the Nuclear Fuel ...ssing Plant (converting ...ons-grade uranium hexafluoride ...inium metal), and the Nuclear ...ponent Manufacturing Plant and ...shop for final weapons assembly.*

Possible *warhead assembly and production facility.*

Headquarters of the North Sea Naval Fleet. *Probable location of China's Xia class ballistic missile nuclear submarine.*

Shangai Institute of Nuclear Research. *Engaged in ballistic missile and nuclear weapons development.*

Chinese Academy of Engineering Physics. *This is a duplicate of the nuclear weapons research and design facility at Haiyan.*

Nuclear Fuel Component Plant. *Used for producing and processing plutonium for nuclear weapons.*

HEILONGJIANG

Harbin

JILIN

Tonghua

NEI MONGOLIA

LIAONING

NORTH KOREA

SOUTH KOREA

Xuanhua

Baotou

Beijing

Dengshahe

Helan Shan

Wuzhai

HEBEI

Tianjin

...atong

NINGXIA

SHANXI

Yidu

SHAN-DONG

Qingdao

Jinan

Lanzhou

Xi'an

HENAN

Luoning

JIANGSU

SHAANXI

Sundian

Guangyuan

ANHUI

Shanghai

Mianyang

CHINA

HUBEI

Lianxiwang

ZHEJIANG

Chengdu

SICHUAN

Heping

Yibin

HUNAN

JIANGXI

FUJIAN

GUIZHOU

Tongdao

Kunming

NAN

Jianshui

GUANGXI

GUANGDONG

TAIWAN

VIETNAM

HONG KONG

East China Sea

AOS

HAINAN

Nuclear Engineering International, October 1993, pp. 16-22.